Y0-CCJ-466

American Beauty

A reminder of who we are, the principles we live by, and an appeal

To Amos, Estelle, Clara, you are all great! Love - Aunt Carolyn Christina + Virginia

George Kalkines

Merry Christmas - 2020

DOWNSTREAM PUBLISHING

NEW YORK · FLORIDA · NORTH CAROLINA

Copyright © 2018 George Kalkines
Cover Photo © 2018 927 Creation / Shutterstock.com
Cover copyright © 2018 George Kalkines
Interior photos unless otherwise noted copyright © 2018 George Kalkines
Presidential and American flag illustrations © 2018 Thomas Hilley
Hardcover endsheet art copyright © 2018 YamabikaY / Shutterstock.com

All Rights Reserved.

In accordance with the U.S. Copyright Act of 1976, scanning, uploading, or electronic sharing of any part of this book, audio, written, or e-published, is strictly prohibited and unlawful. No part of this book may be reproduced in any form or by any means, including photocopying, electronic, mechanical, recording, or by any information storage and retrieval system without permission in writing by the copyright owner.

Downstream Publishing, LLC
241 Chimney Lane
Wilmington, NC 28409
www.DownstreamPublishing.com

FIRST EDITION PRINTED OCTOBER 2018
Printed in the USA.

Library of Congress Control Number: 2018954778

ISBN-13: 978-1-7326406-0-3 *American Beauty* Hardcover
ISBN-13: 978-1-7326406-1-0 *American Beauty* Softcover

10 9 8 7 6 5 4 3 2 1

This book is dedicated:

To our fellow citizens, with a hope for their continued commitment to fulfilling
the promise of America by living each day in accordance with the
fundamental principles and freedoms envisioned by our founders and defined by our laws.

To our men and women who have sacrificed their lives, who have suffered serious injuries,
and those who have served and continue to serve in our armed forces to preserve our principles.

To two little people, my granddaughters, Elisabeth "Bee" and Penelope "Poppy,"
who are three years old, and who, like millions of other children in America,
hopefully will learn and live by these principles.

And to Ann.

. . . .

*Ten percent of the profits from the sales of this book
will be shared equally among various veterans organizations.*

The Reminder

The current state of affairs in our country compels us as a people, individually and collectively, to take a moment to remember who we are and what we mutually believe the essential elements and guiding principles of our nation to be, now and as we go forward.

It is not the extraordinary beauty of the American Beauty Rose or the magnificence of the soaring American Bald Eagle but rather the basic precepts of our nation's principles that have provided the critical framework for our democracy.

These are the principles that are embodied in our founding documents, the historic quotes of our leaders as we evolved as a nation, and even the prose, poetry, and lyrics of our nation's writers and composers.

Let us resolve to be guided by these ideals of social and economic freedom and justice with a particular emphasis on our collective generosity and our commitment to improving the quality of life for all Americans.

Let us bring these principles back into focus and move away from the political polarization and divisiveness that have gripped our nation in recent decades.

Our philosophical, political, and economic underpinnings have permitted us to lead the world since our inception as a nation in 1776. Because of these same principles, throughout our history we have been the hope of the world. Let us not abandon that leadership. Let us remember we are a blessed people.

"Let us not despair but act. Let us not seek the Republican answer or the Democratic answer but the right answer. Let us not seek to fix the blame for the past—let us accept our own responsibility for the future."

—President John F. Kennedy

KAREN ROACH / SHUTTERSTOCK.COM

I PLEDGE ALLEGIANCE

TO THE FLAG OF THE

UNITED STATES OF AMERICA

AND TO THE REPUBLIC FOR WHICH IT STANDS,

ONE NATION UNDER GOD, INDIVISIBLE,

WITH LIBERTY AND JUSTICE FOR ALL

The U.S. Pledge of Allegiance as we know it was written in August 1892 by Francis Bellamy, the son of a Baptist minister from upstate New York, who wrote it as part of his duties in the promotions department of The Youth's Companion *magazine. Bellamy wrote it to be recited in fifteen seconds. In 1923, the words "the flag of the United States of America" replaced "my flag." In 1954, in response to the Communist threat hanging like a shadow over the world, President Eisenhower encouraged Congress to add the words "under God."*

Introduction

The American Flag and the Pledge of Allegiance

The flag of our nation represents our cohesiveness as a people and the embodiment of our nation's principles.

The Pledge of Allegiance represents a reaffirmation of our individual and collective commitment to that cohesiveness and the principles we hold dear, most notably freedom, justice, equality, and opportunity. These principles are as sacred as any religious credo.

In the past, every child who attended public school was required to memorize the Pledge of Allegiance and then recite it at the start of each school day.

As grown-ups when the occasion arises, we repeat the Pledge by rote memory. The Pledge was indistinct in our minds and hearts from the other rituals that we as Americans shared and engaged in when called upon to express our patriotism.

Regrettably, recent reports indicate fewer and fewer children and adults know the Pledge, much less understand it. What has been lost is an understanding of what it truly means to *pledge our allegiance* to our country.

The purpose of this book is to offer a brief review of our history and our leaders—both past and present including their words and actions, with the hope that it will cause us to remember and understand what it means to be a citizen of the United States of America.

We gain greater appreciation for the Pledge of Allegiance by placing it against the backdrop of the development of our country, the events that shaped it, and the prose, poetry, and lyrics that our fellow Americans have written to capture the extraordinary principles that have been the cornerstones of our nation's foundation and have guided our leaders and our people throughout its history.

These principles are worth repeating and keeping in the forefront of our minds as we recite the Pledge of Allegiance and come together to both preserve our freedoms and address the complex issues and problems of our times.

"We hold these truths to be self-evident, that all men are created equal, that they are endowed by their Creator with certain unalienable Rights, that among these are Life, Liberty and the pursuit of Happiness."

—Thomas Jefferson, from the Declaration of Independence

I pledge ...

GEORGE KALKINES

Birthplace of a Great Nation
Independence Hall, Philadelphia, Pennsylvania, July 4, 1776

DAN THORNBERG / SHUTTERSTOCK.COM

We the People of the United States,
in Order to form a more perfect Union, establish Justice, insure domestic Tranquility,
provide for the common defence, promote the general Welfare, and secure the Blessings of Liberty to ourselves
and our Posterity, do ordain and establish this Constitution for the United States of America.

allegiance ...

"Proclaim LIBERTY throughout all the Land unto all the Inhabitants thereof"
—Leviticus 25:10 as inscribed on the Liberty Bell

"As the British Constitution is the most subtle organism which has proceeded from the womb and long gestation of progressive history, so the American Constitution is, so far as I can see, the most wonderful work ever struck off at a given time by the brain and purpose of man."
—W. E. Gladstone, British prime minister

If I Had a Hammer
. . . Well, I've got a hammer
And I've got a bell
And I've got a song to sing
All over this land
It's the hammer of justice
It's the bell of freedom
It's a song about love between
My brothers and my sisters
All over this land. . . .
　Lyrics: Pete Seeger and Lee Hays, 1949

SONGQUAN DENG / SHUTTERSTOCK.COM

Let Freedom Ring
Liberty Bell, Philadelphia; opposite, U.S. Constitution

The Bill of Rights

Amendment I. Congress shall make no law respecting an establishment of religion, or prohibiting the free exercise thereof; or abridging the freedom of speech, or of the press; or the right of the people peaceably to assemble, and to petition the Government for a redress of grievances.

Amendment II. A well regulated Militia, being necessary to the security of a free State, the right of the people to keep and bear Arms, shall not be infringed.

Amendment III. No Soldier shall, in time of peace be quartered in any house, without the consent of the Owner, nor in time of war, but in a manner to be prescribed by law.

Amendment IV. The right of the people to be secure in their persons, houses, papers, and effects, against unreasonable searches and seizures, shall not be violated, and no Warrants shall issue, but upon probable cause, supported by Oath or affirmation, and particularly describing the place to be searched, and the persons or things to be seized.

Amendment V. No person shall be held to answer for a capital, or otherwise infamous crime, unless on a presentment or indictment of a Grand Jury, except in cases arising in the land or naval forces, or in the Militia, when in actual service in time of War or public danger; nor shall any person be subject for the same offence to be twice put in jeopardy of life or limb; nor shall be compelled in any criminal case to be a witness against himself, nor be deprived of life, liberty, or property, without due process of law; nor shall private property be taken for public use, without just compensation.

Amendment VI. In all criminal prosecutions, the accused shall enjoy the right to a speedy and public trial, by an impartial jury of the State and district wherein the crime shall have been committed, which district shall have been previously ascertained by law, and to be informed of the nature and cause of the accusation; to be confronted with the witnesses against him; to have compulsory process for obtaining witnesses in his favor, and to have the Assistance of Counsel for his defence.

Amendment VII. In Suits at common law, where the value in controversy shall exceed twenty dollars, the right of trial by jury shall be preserved, and no fact tried by a jury, shall be otherwise re-examined in any Court of the United States, than according to the rules of the common law.

Amendment VIII. Excessive bail shall not be required, nor excessive fines imposed, nor cruel and unusual punishments inflicted.

Amendment IX. The enumeration in the Constitution, of certain rights, shall not be construed to deny or disparage others retained by the people.

Amendment X. The powers not delegated to the United States by the Constitution, nor prohibited by it to the States, are reserved to the States respectively, or to the people.

"The liberty of the press is essential to the security of freedom in a state. . . ."
— **John Adams, 1780, Constitution of the Commonwealth of Massachusetts**

to the Flag ...

"Whoever would overthrow the Liberty of a nation, must begin by subduing the Freeness of Speech."

—**Benjamin Franklin, 1722**

"There is nothing so fretting and vexatious, nothing so justly Terrible to tyrants, and their tools and abettors, as a Free Press."

—**Samuel Adams, 1768**

"A popular Government, without popular information, or the means of acquiring it, is but a Prologue to a Farce or a Tragedy; or, perhaps both. Knowledge will forever govern ignorance: And a people who mean to be their own Governors, must arm themselves with the power which knowledge gives."

—**James Madison, 1822**

". . . there is a terrific disadvantage not having the abrasive quality of the press applied to you daily, to an administration, even though we never like it, and even though we wish they didn't write it, and even though we disapprove, there isn't any doubt that we could not do the job at all in a free society without a very, very active press."

—**President John F. Kennedy, 1962**

GEORGE KALKINES

The Stars and Stripes
Betsy Ross House, Philadelphia, Pennsylvania

From George Washington's Farewell Address of 1796

. . . The unity of government which constitutes you one people is also now dear to you. It is justly so, for it is a main pillar in the edifice of your real independence, the support of your tranquility at home, your peace abroad; of your safety; of your prosperity; of that very liberty which you so highly prize.

But as it is easy to foresee that, from different causes and from different quarters, much pains will be taken, many artifices employed, to weaken in your minds the conviction of this truth; as this is the point in your political fortress against which the batteries of internal and external enemies will be most constantly and actively (though often covertly and insidiously) directed, it is of infinite moment that you should properly estimate the immense value of your national union to your collective and individual happiness; that you should cherish a cordial, habitual, and immovable attachment to it; accustoming yourselves to think and speak of it as of the palladium of your political safety and prosperity; watching for its preservation with jealous anxiety; discountenancing whatever may suggest even a suspicion that it can in any event be abandoned; and indignantly frowning upon the first dawning of every attempt to alienate any portion of our country from the rest, or to enfeeble the sacred ties which now link together the various parts.

For this you have every inducement of sympathy and interest. Citizens, by birth or choice, of a common country, that country has a right to concentrate your affections. The name of American, which belongs to you in your national capacity, must always exalt the just pride of patriotism more than any appellation derived from local discriminations. . . .

". . . [if] the freedom of Speech may be taken away—and, dumb & silent we may be led, like sheep, to the Slaughter."
— **President George Washington, 1783**

"There is no more essential ingredient than a free, strong, and independent press to our continued success in what the Founding Fathers called our 'noble experiment' in self-government."
— **President Ronald Reagan, 1983**

"I consider the media to be indispensable to democracy. We need the media to hold people like me to account. Power can be very addictive, and it can be corrosive. It's important for the media to call to account people who abuse their power, whether it be here or elsewhere."
— **President George W. Bush, 2017**

of the
United States ...

As far back as 1783, there was a call for a monument to honor George Washington, the leader of the Continental army during the American Revolution, the presiding officer over the convention that drafted the U.S. Constitution, and the first President of the United States.

By 1848, the Monument Society had collected enough money to fund the project, selected an architect and design, and laid the cornerstone, but the Washington Monument would not be finished for another thirty-eight years as political turmoil and uncertainty about the survival of the American Union brought construction to a halt.

When completed in 1884, it was the tallest building in the world at 555 feet and five-eighth inches. Dedicated on February 21, 1885, it officially opened to the public on October 9, 1888.

Fifty American flags—one for each of the country's fifty states—now ring the base of the monument.

GEORGE KALKINES

Standing Tall Forever
Washington Monument, Washington, D.C.

"Guard against the impostures of pretended patriotism."

—George Washington

". . . I have sworn upon the altar of God eternal, hostility against every form of tyranny over the mind of man."

—Thomas Jefferson

". . . honesty is the 1st chapter in the book of wisdom."

—Thomas Jefferson

"A house divided against itself cannot stand."

—Abraham Lincoln

"Let reverence for the laws, be breathed by every American mother, to the lisping babe, that prattles on her lap—let it be taught in schools, in seminaries, and in colleges; let it be written in Primers, spelling books, and in Almanacs;—let it be preached from the pulpit, proclaimed in legislative halls, and enforced in courts of justice. And, in short, let it become the political religion of the nation; and let the old and the young, the rich and the poor, the grave and the gay, of all sexes and tongues, and colors and conditions, sacrifice unceasingly upon its altars."

—Abraham Lincoln

"In the first place, we should insist that if the immigrant who comes here in good faith becomes an American and assimilates himself to us, he shall be treated on an exact equality with everyone else, for it is an outrage to discriminate against any such man because of creed, or birthplace, or origin."

—Theodore Roosevelt

# of America ...

What foresight! What wisdom! What leadership! Thoughts so profound they have provided us with 242 years of guidance.

It took four hundred people from October 4, 1927, to October 31, 1941, to create Mount Rushmore.

The purpose of the memorial is to "communicate the founding, expansion, preservation, and unification of the United States," according to its American sculptor John Gutzon.

GEORGE KALKINES

Leadership
Mount Rushmore, Keystone, South Dakota

The Words of Ulysses S. Grant, General and President

"Though I have been trained as a soldier, and participated in many battles, there never was a time when, in my opinion, some way could not be found to prevent the drawing of the sword. I look forward to an epoch when a court, recognized by all nations, will settle international differences, instead of keeping large standing armies as they do in Europe."

"I don't know why black skin may not cover a true heart as well as a white one."

"There are but two parties now: traitors and patriots, and I want hereafter to be ranked with the latter and, I trust, the stronger party."

"If we are to have another contest in the near future of our national existence I predict that the dividing line will not be Mason and Dixon's, but between patriotism and intelligence on the one side and superstition, ambition and ignorance on the other."

"Whatever there is of greatness in the United States, or indeed in any other country, is due to labor. The laborer is the author of all greatness and wealth. Without labor there would be no government, no leading class, and nothing to preserve."

"Let us labor for the security of free thought, free speech, pure morals, unfettered religious sentiments, and equal rights and privileges for all men, irrespective of nationality, color, or religion. . . . Leave the matter of religious teaching to the family altar, the church, and the private school, supported entirely by private contribution. Keep church and state forever separate."

and to the Republic ...

"Let us have peace."
— **General Ulysses S. Grant**

". . . I never heard him abuse an enemy. Some of the cruel things said about President Lincoln, particularly in the North, used to pierce him to the heart; but never in my presence did he evince a revengeful disposition. . . . "
— **General Ulysses S. Grant**

GEORGE KALKINES

A Soaring Purpose
Grant's Tomb, General Grant National Memorial, New York City, N.Y.

Hymns of the Armed Forces

Marine Corps Hymn

(U.S. Marine Corps, revised 1942)

From the Halls of Montezuma
To the Shores of Tripoli;
We fight our country's battles
In the air, on land, and sea;
First to fight for right and freedom
And to keep our honor clean;
We are proud to claim the title
of United States Marine.

Wild Blue Yonder

(U.S. Air Force)

Off we go into the wild blue yonder,
Climbing high into the sun;
Here they come zooming to meet our thunder,
At 'em boys, Give 'er the gun! (Give 'er the gun now!)
Down we dive, spouting our flame from under,
Off with one helluva roar!
We live in fame or go down in flame. Hey!
Nothing'll stop the U.S. Air Force!

Anchors Aweigh

(U.S. Navy, revised 1997)

Anchors Aweigh, my boys, Anchors Aweigh.
Farewell to foreign shores, we sail at break of day-ay-ay-ay.
Through our last night on ashore, drink to the foam,
Until we meet once more,
Here's wishing you a happy voyage home.

The Army Goes Rolling Along

(U.S. Army, official song 1956)

March along, sing our song,
With the Army of the free
Count the brave, count the true,
Who have fought to victory
We're the Army and proud of our name
We're the Army and proudly proclaim

Refrain:
Then it's Hi! Hi! Hey!
The Army's on its way.
Count off the cadence loud and strong,
For where e'er we go,
You will always know
That The Army Goes Rolling Along.

Semper Paratus

(U.S. Coast Guard)

From North and South and East and West,
The Coast Guard's in the fight.
Destroying subs and landing troops,
The Axis feels our might.
For we're the first invaders,
On every fighting field.
Afloat, ashore, on men and Spars,
You'll find the Coast Guard shield.

for which ...

GEORGE KALKINES

Freedom for People Everywhere
U.S. Marine Corps War Memorial, Arlington, Virginia

"Our debt to the heroic men and valiant women in the service of our country can never be repaid.
They have earned our undying gratitude. America will never forget their sacrifices. Because of these sacrifices,
the dawn of justice and freedom throughout the world slowly casts its gleam across the horizon."

—Harry S. Truman

"They fought together as brothers in arms; they died together and now they sleep side by side.
To them, we have a solemn obligation—the obligation to ensure that their sacrifice
will help make this a better and safer world in which to live."

—Admiral Chester W. Nimitz

"We are determined that before the sun sets on this terrible struggle, Our Flag will be recognized throughout
the World as a symbol of Freedom on the one hand and of overwhelming force on the other."

—General George Marshall

"Believe me when I say that laughter up at the front lines is a very precious thing—precious to those grand guys
who are giving and taking the awful business that goes on there. . . . There's a lump the size of Grant's Tomb
in your throat when they come up to you and shake your hand and mumble 'Thanks.'
Imagine those guys thanking me! Look what they're doin' for me. And for you."

—Bob Hope

it stands ...

JEREMY R. SMITH, JR. / SHUTTERSTOCK.com

Eternal Companion
Arlington Cemetery, Virginia

FDR's 'Four Freedoms' Speech

. . . The basic things expected by our people of their political and economic systems are simple. They are: Equality of opportunity for youth and for others. Jobs for those who can work. Security for those who need it. The ending of special privilege for the few. The preservation of civil liberties for all. The enjoyment—the enjoyment of the fruits of scientific progress in a wider and constantly rising standard of living. These are the simple, the basic things that must never be lost sight of in the turmoil and unbelievable complexity of our modern world. The inner and abiding strength of our economic and political systems is dependent upon the degree to which they fulfill these expectations.

Many subjects connected with our social economy call for immediate improvement. As examples: We should bring more citizens under the coverage of old-age pensions and unemployment insurance. We should widen the opportunities for adequate medical care. We should plan a better system by which persons deserving or needing gainful employment may obtain it. I have called for personal sacrifice. And I am assured of the willingness of almost all Americans to respond to that call. A part of the sacrifice means the payment of more money in taxes. In my Budget Message I will recommend that a greater portion of this great defense program be paid for from taxation than we are paying for today. No person should try, or be allowed to get rich out of the program; and the principle of tax payments in accordance with ability to pay should be constantly before our eyes to guide our legislation. If the Congress maintains these principles the voters, putting patriotism ahead of pocketbooks, will give you their applause.

In the future days, which we seek to make secure, we look forward to a world founded upon four essential human freedoms. The first is freedom of speech and expression—everywhere in the world. The second is freedom of every person to worship God in his own way—everywhere in the world. The third is freedom from want—which, translated into world terms, means economic understandings which will secure to every nation a healthy peacetime life for its inhabitants—everywhere in the world. The fourth is freedom from fear—which, translated into world terms, means a world-wide reduction of armaments to such a point and in such a thorough fashion that no nation will be in a position to commit an act of physical aggression against any neighbor—anywhere in the world.

That is no vision of a distant millennium. It is a definite basis for a kind of world attainable in our own time and generation. That kind of world is the very antithesis of the so-called new order of tyranny which the dictators seek to create with the crash of a bomb. To that new order we oppose the greater conception—the moral order. A good society is able to face schemes of world domination and foreign revolutions alike without fear. Since the beginning of our American history we have been engaged in change—in a perpetual, peaceful revolution—a revolution which goes on steadily, quietly, adjusting itself to changing conditions—without the concentration camp or the quicklime in the ditch. The world order which we seek is the cooperation of free countries, working together in a friendly, civilized society.

This nation has placed its destiny in the hands and heads and hearts of its millions of free men and women; and its faith in freedom under the guidance of God. Freedom means the supremacy of human rights everywhere. Our support goes to those who struggle to gain those rights and keep them. Our strength is our unity of purpose. To that high concept there can be no end save victory.

—Franklin Delano Roosevelt, January 6, 1941

GEORGE KALKINES

one nation ...

THEY (WHO) SEEK TO ESTABLISH
SYSTEMS OF GOVERNMENT BASED ON
THE REGIMENTATION OF ALL HUMAN
BEINGS BY A HANDFUL OF INDIVIDUAL
RULERS... CALL THIS A NEW ORDER.
IT IS NOT NEW AND IT IS NOT ORDER.

A New Deal for the People
Franklin Delano Roosevelt Memorial, Washington, D.C.

Songs of our Nation

The Star-Spangled Banner

O say can you see, by the dawn's early light,
What so proudly we hail'd at the twilight's last gleaming,
Whose broad stripes and bright stars through the perilous fight
O'er the ramparts we watch'd were so gallantly streaming?
And the rocket's red glare, the bomb bursting in air,
Gave proof through the night that our flag was still there,
O say does that star-spangled banner yet wave
O'er the land of the free and the home of the brave?

Lyrics: Francis Scott Keys

America the Beautiful

O beautiful for spacious skies,
For amber waves of grain,
For purple mountain magesties
Above the fruited plain!
America! America!
God shed His grace on thee
And crown thy good with brotherhood
From sea to shining sea!

Lyrics: Katharine Lee Bates

You're a Grand Old Flag

(Chorus)
You're a grand old flag,
You're a high flying flag
And forever in peace may you wave.
You're the emblem of
The land I love.
The home of the free and the brave.
Ev'ry heart beats true
'neath the Red, White and Blue,
Where there's never a boast or brag.
But should auld acquaintance be forgot,
Keep your eye on the grand old flag.

Lyrics: George M. Cohan

God Bless America

God bless America, land that I love
Stand beside her and guide her
Through the night with the light from above
From the mountains to the prairies
To the oceans white with foam
God bless America, my home sweet home
From the mountains to the prairies
To the oceans white with foam
God bless America, my home sweet home
God bless America, my home sweet home

Lyrics: Irving Berlin

"God Bless America" lyrics © Peermusic Publishing

under God ...

"We identify the flag with almost everything we hold dear on earth. It represents our peace and security, our civil and political liberty, our freedom of worship, our family, our friends, our home. . . . But when we look at our flag and behold it emblazoned with all our rights we must remember that it is equally a symbol of our duties. Every glory that we associate with it is the result of duty done. . . ."

—Calvin Coolidge

BRO CREATIVE / SHUTTERSTOCK.COM

Blessed
A symbol of our duties

The Gettysburg Address

Four score and seven years ago our fathers brought forth, upon this continent, a new nation, conceived in Liberty, and dedicated to the proposition that all men are created equal.

Now we are engaged in a great civil war, testing whether that nation, or any nation so conceived and so dedicated, can long endure. We are met on a great battlefield of that war. We have come to dedicate a portion of that field, as a final resting place for those who here gave their lives that that nation might live. It is altogether fitting and proper that we should do this.

But, in a larger sense, we cannot dedicate—we cannot consecrate—we cannot hallow—this ground. The brave men, living and dead, who struggled here have consecrated it, far above our poor power to add or detract. The world will little note, nor long remember what we say here, but it can never forget what they did here. It is for us the living, rather, to be dedicated here to the unfinished work which they who fought here have thus far so nobly advanced. It is rather for us to be here dedicated to the great task remaining before us—that from these honored dead we take increased devotion to that cause for which they gave the last full measure of devotion—that we here highly resolve that these dead shall not have died in vain—that this nation, under God, shall have a new birth of freedom—and that government of the people, by the people, for the people, shall not perish from the earth.

—Abraham Lincoln, November 19, 1863

From Lincoln's final autographed manuscript of the Gettysburg Address known as the "Bliss Copy." It hangs in the White House and is considered to be the most authoritative text of the speech.

indivisible ...

"With malice toward none; with charity for all; with firmness in the right, as God gives us to see the right, let us strive on to finish the work we are in; to bind up the nation's wounds; to care for him who shall have borne the battle, and for his widow, and his orphan—to do all which may achieve and cherish a just and lasting peace, among ourselves, and with all nations."

—President Abraham Lincoln, second inaugural address, March 4, 1865

ORHAN CAM / SHUTTERSTOCK.com

Indivisible
Lincoln Memorial, Washington, D.C.

The Statue of Liberty

Give me your tired, your poor, your huddled
masses yearning to breathe free, the wretched
refuse of your teeming shore. Send these,
the homeless, tempest-tossed to me, I lift
my lamp beside the golden door!

—Inscription, Statue of Liberty

These lines from the poem *The New Colossus*, written by Emma Lazarus in 1883, grace the *Statue of Liberty* that stands on Liberty Island in New York Harbor. A symbol of the alliance formed between France and the young American republic during the Revolutionary War, the 151-foot statue was originally intended to mark the centennial anniversary of the Declaration of Independence in 1887. However, it arrived early in June of 1885.

Designed by the sculptor Frederic Auguste Bartholdi, with an iron framework by Gustave Eiffel (the man who designed the Eiffel Tower in Paris, France), it took nine years with crews working seven days a week, around the clock, to complete. The statue was then disassembled into 350 pieces and shipped to New York City, where it took four months for it to be put back together.

It was officially unveiled and dedicated on October 28, 1886. Originally named *Liberty Enlightening the World*, it is now known simply as the *Statue of Liberty*.

with Liberty ...

"... We will not forget that liberty has here made her home, nor shall her chosen altar be neglected."

—Grover Cleveland,
1886 dedication of the
Statue of Liberty

"We don't want an America that is closed to the world. What we want is a world that is open to America."

—George H.W. Bush

"... for the United States of America, there will be no forgetting September the 11th. We will remember every rescuer who died in honor. We will remember every family that lives in grief. We will remember the fire and ash, the last phone calls, the funerals of the children."

—George W. Bush

GEORGE KALKINES

Yearning to be Free
Statue of Liberty and the World Trade Center's Twin Towers, NYC, N.Y.

"I think the first duty of society is justice."
—**Alexander Hamilton**

"I hate to hear people say this Judge will vote so and so, because he is a Democrat—and this one so and so because he is a Republican. It is shameful. The Judges have the Constitution for their guidance; they have no right to any politics save the politics of rigid right and justice when they are sitting in judgment upon the great matters that come before them."
—**Mark Twain**

"It is emphatically the province and duty of the judicial department to say what the law is."
—**John Marshall on** *Marbury v. Madison*, **1803**

"History teaches that grave threats to liberty often come in times of urgency, when constitutional rights seem too extravagant to endure."
—**Thurgood Marshall**

"Many people consider the things government does for them to be social progress but they regard the things government does for others as socialism."
—**Earl Warren**

"If our free society is to endure, and I know it will, those who govern must recognize that the Framers of the Constitution limited their power in order to preserve human dignity and the air of freedom which is our proudest heritage. The task of protecting these principles does not rest solely with nine Supreme Court Justices, or even with the cadre of state and federal judges. We all share the burden."
—**William Brennan**

"We shall overcome, We shall overcome, We shall overcome, some day."
—**"We Shall Overcome"**

and Justice ...

ORHAN CAM / SHUTTERSTOCK.COM

Ultimate Arbiter

U.S. Supreme Court, Washington, D.C.

"This land is your land, this land is my land
From California to the New York Island
From the Redwood Forest, to the Gulf stream waters
This land was made for you and me."
**—"This Land is Your Land,"
by Woody Guthrie**

"We will never have true civilization until we have learned to recognize the rights of others."
—Will Rogers

"The ultimate measure of a man is not where he stands in moments of comfort and convenience,
but where he stands in times of challenge and controversy."
—Martin Luther King Jr.

"There never will be complete equality until women themselves help to make laws and elect lawmakers."
—Susan B. Anthony

"A good leader inspires people to have confidence in the leader.
A great leader inspires people to have confidence in themselves."
—Eleanor Roosevelt

for all.

"We defend and we build a way of life,
not for America alone, but for all mankind."
—Franklin D. Roosevelt,
   fireside chat on national defense,
   May 26, 1940

"The vote is the emblem of your equality,
women of America, the guarantee of your liberty.
That vote of yours has cost millions of dollars
and the lives of thousands of women. Money to
carry on this work has been given usually as a
sacrifice, and thousands of women have gone
without things they wanted and could have had
in order that they might help get the vote for you.
Women have suffered agony of soul which you
can never comprehend, that you and your
daughters might inherit political freedom. That
vote has been costly. Prize it! The vote is a
power, a weapon of offense and defense, a prayer.
Understand what it means and what it can do
for your country. Use it intelligently,
conscientiously, prayerfully."
—Carrie Chapman Catt, suffragette and
   founder of the League of Women Voters

GEORGE KALKINES

Of the People, For the People, By the People
U.S. Capitol, Washington, D.C.

The Presidents
& Old Glory

The Birth of Old Glory *by Edward Mercy Moran*

THE LIBRARY OF CONGRESS

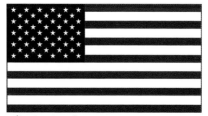
The American flag

The Evolution of the American Flag
and the Presidents Who Served under It

Red: for valor and hardiness

White: for purity and innocence

Blue: for vigilance, perseverance, and justice

Stars: in a circle so that no colony would be viewed above another.

The Betsy Ross Flag, designed with thirteen stars and thirteen stripes to represent
the thirteen colonies—Virginia (1607), New York (1626), Massachusetts (1630),
Maryland (1633), Rhode Island (1636), Connecticut (1636), New Hampshire (1638),
Delaware (1638), North Carolina (1653), South Carolina (1663), New Jersey (1664),
Pennsylvania (1682), and Georgia (1732), became the first official flag of the United States in 1777.

Initially, Congress did not specify dimensions, proportions, shapes, or star patterns, so
flags varied dramatically. According to legend, Betsy Ross designed and sewed
the first American flag, but most historians now believe the designer to be Francis Hopkinson.

The Second Continental Congress passed the Flag Resolution of 1777 on June 14, 1777,
making the Betsy Ross Flag official. This date is now celebrated annually as Flag Day.

Betsy Ross flag, first official flag of the United States of America—Washington is the only president to serve under this flag: 1777–1795.

George Washington

1. George Washington

(1732–1799)

Presidency: 1789–1797 | Two terms | 18th century

Vice President: John Adams

"Knowledge is in every country the surest basis of public happiness."

How He Defined the Office:

Washington established the two-term tradition of the presidency.

Accomplishments & Failures:

* Selected the location of the nation's capital

* Established a presidency instead of answering the call to become king

* The Bill of Rights, which includes the first ten Amendments to the U.S. Constitution, ratified December 15, 1791

* 1795 Treaty of Greenville ended Indian Wars in Ohio and opened area for settlement; established U.S. western border

* 1795 Pickney's Treaty signed with Spain; fixed the southern boundary of the U.S.; granted U.S. ships the right to free navigation of the Mississippi River

* Judiciary Act of 1789 established six-member U.S. Supreme Court, position of attorney general

* Naturalization Act of 1790 established rules for granting citizenship

* Bank Act of 1791 created the First Bank of the United States

* Excise Tax on Whiskey, 1791, levied federal tax to offset government's assumption of some state debts

* Militia Acts of 1792 created more uniform and regulated militia structure

* Established a position of neutrality for the United States in regard to foreign affairs

* A slave owner who didn't free his slaves during his lifetime, Washington's will freed them upon the death of his wife. The couple was childless.

Star-Spangled Banner flag, with fifteen stars and fifteen stripes; it represents the thirteen original states plus Kentucky and Vermont: 1795–1818.

2. John Adams

(1735–1826)

Presidency: 1797–1801 | One term | 18th & 19th centuries

Vice President: Thomas Jefferson

"Facts are stubborn things; and whatever may be our wishes, our inclinations, or the dictates of our passions, they cannot alter the state of facts and evidence."

John Adams

How He Defined the Office:

Adams saw foreign policy as the President's bailiwick, while Congress dealt with domestic policy.

Accomplishments & Failures:

* 11th Amendment ratified February 7, 1795; limited the jurisdiction of federal courts

* U.S. Department of the Navy created

* Alien and Sedition Acts signed into law in 1798; allowed for detention of enemy aliens without a trial

* Federal Bankruptcy Act signed into law 1800; limited to traders and provided only for involuntary proceedings

* Library of Congress established in 1800; $5,000 appropriated to purchase books

* Divided Northwest Territory: Ohio and East Michigan retained name; Indiana, West Michigan, and East Wisconsin became Indiana Territory.

· ·

Thomas Jefferson

3. Thomas Jefferson

(1743–1826)

Presidency: 1801–1809 | Two terms | 19th century

Vice Presidents: Aaron Burr (1801–1805), George Clinton (1805–1809)

"In matters of style, swim with the current; in matters of principle, stand like a rock."

How He Defined the Office:

Jefferson did not believe in strong central government yet used the full force of the office when necessary.

Accomplishments & Failures:

* War with Tripoli declared over U.S.'s refusal to pay more tribute to Tripoli for protection from piracy; authorized arming of merchant ships

* Enabling Act of 1802 passed, calling for the admittance of Ohio as a state

* 1803 Louisiana Purchase purchased 827,000 square miles of French land between Mississippi River and Rockies for $15 million

* 1804 Lewis and Clark Expedition saw his personal secretary Meriwether Lewis and William Clark sent to explore the West and find water passage to Pacific

* 12th Amendment ratified June 15, 1804; required separate vote for President and Vice President

* Act Prohibiting Importation of Slaves of 1807 forbade any new slaves to be imported into United States.

James Madison

4. James Madison
(1751–1836)
Presidency: 1809–1817 | Two terms | 19th century
Vice Presidents: George Clinton (1809–1812), none (1812–1813),
Elbridge Gerry (1813–1814), none (1814–1817)

"If men were angels, no government would be necessary."

How He Defined the Office:

Madison pushed using checks and balances to limit government power further than anyone else had to date, but when the U.S. declared war on Great Britain in June 1812, the conflict was nicknamed "Mr. Madison's War."

Accomplishments & Failures:

* Non-Intercourse Act of 1809 reduced trade embargoes on American shipping except for those bound for British or French ports
* War of 1812: In response to U.S. policy not to trade with England, British seized American ships and set fire to White House in August 1814
* Proclamation to Occupy West Florida
* Bank of the United States closed in 1816; signed bill rechartering the bank for a twenty-one-year term
* Treaty of Ghent ended the war with England following U.S. victory over British in the Battle of New Orleans 1815
* The Tariff of 1816: first actual protectionist measure in United States; passed to protect U.S. manufactured items from overseas competition
* Second Bank of the United States in 1816: despite long opposing a national bank, chartered a new federal bank for a twenty-year term.

· ·

20-star American flag, also known as the Great Star Flag and the Flag of 1818. Congress passed the Flag Act of 1818, adding five new stars (Tennessee, Ohio, Louisiana, Indiana, Mississippi) and reducing the stripes to thirteen: 1818–1819.

21-star American flag (Illinois): 1819–1820.

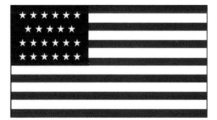

23-star American flag (Alabama and Maine): 1820–1822.

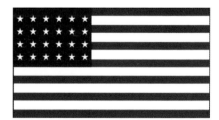

24-star American flag (Missouri), Old Glory name adopted: 1822–1836.

5. James Monroe
(1758–1831)
Presidency: 1817–1825 | Two terms | 19th century
Vice President: Daniel D. Thompkins (1817–1825)

"The best form of government is that ... which is most likely to prevent the greatest sum of evil."

James Monroe

How He Defined the Office:

Monroe embraced two policies that would define America's future—one with regard to the expansion of slavery, the other to the Western hemisphere as it pertained to European meddling.

Accomplishments & Failures:

* Era of Good Feelings: presided over a period that started in 1815 and was defined by a sense of national purpose and unity in the wake of the Napoleonic Wars and the War of 1812; name was coined by a Boston journalist
* Treaty of 1818 established the boundary between the United States and Canadian territories at the 49th parallel
* Panic of 1819: first major peacetime financial crisis
* Monroe Doctrine declared the United States would no longer tolerate European interference in the Western hemisphere
* Missouri Compromise admitted Missouri as slave state and Maine as free state; prohibited slavery in Louisiana Territory north of 36° 30' latitude.

. . . .

6. John Quincy Adams
(1767–1848)
Presidency: 1825–1829 | One term | 19th century
Vice President: John C. Calhoun (1825–1829)

"Always vote for principle, though you may vote alone, and you may cherish the sweetest reflection that your vote is never lost."

John Quincy Adams

How He Defined the Office:

Adams believed in a strong federal government and the role of the President to help improve societal conditions.

Accomplishments & Failures:

* U.S. Naval Observatory: signed bill to create observatory as part of his efforts as a champion of the arts and sciences
* Tariff of 1828 Act set high duties on goods imported into the United States
* Erie Canal completed in 1825
* Baltimore and Ohio Railroad begun in 1828.

Andrew Jackson

7. Andrew Jackson
(1767–1845)
Presidency: 1829–1837 | Two terms | 19th century
Vice Presidents: John C. Calhoun (1829–1832), none (1832–1833), Martin Van Buren (1833–1837)

"There are no necessary evils in government. Its evils exist only in its abuses."

How He Defined the Office:
Jackson is credited with inspiring the two-party system; he vetoed twelve bills—more than any previous President, and his practice of giving his cronies political positions introduced the "spoils system" to American politics.

Accomplishments & Failures:
* Indian Removal Act of 1830: sided with Georgia ownership of tribal lands; removed and relocated tribes out west, creating what became known as the Trail of Tears, named by the Choctaw—in which thousands of Cherokee, Chickasaws, Choctaws, Creeks, and Seminoles died during removal over several years on various routes, both inland and water
* Tariff of 1832, Force Bill authorized President to use armed force to enforce federal tariff laws
* 1835 assassination attempt thwarted
* Panic of 1837: vetoed charter for Second Bank of the United States; took money out and put it in coffers of state banks, which lent it without due diligence, leading to inflation; Jackson's response was the Specie Act, which required land purchases be made in silver or gold, which led to the Panic of 1837.

25-star American flag (Arkansas): 1836–1837.

Martin Van Buren

8. Martin Van Buren
(1782–1862)
Presidency: 1837–1841 | One term | 19th century
Vice President: Richard M. Johnson (1837–1841)

"The government should not be guided by temporary excitement, but by sober second thought."

How He Defined the Office:
Van Buren was the first President born an American citizen, not a British subject.

26-star American flag (Michigan): 1837–1845.

Accomplishments & Failures:
* Panic of 1937: faced almost immediately upon taking office; it was the worst financial crisis America had faced in its short history
* Caroline Affair: Canadian militia set American steamer, *Caroline*, afire and sent it over Niagara Falls, almost starting a war with Britain
* Blocked annexation of Texas.

9. William Henry Harrison
(1773–1841)
Presidency: 1841 | One partial term | 19th century
Vice President: John Tyler (1841)

"The only legitimate right to govern is an express grant of power from the governed."

How He Defined the Office:

Harrison had no chance to leave a mark; he held the office only for thirty-two days—the shortest tenure ever for a President.

William Henry Harrison

Accomplishments & Failures:

* At age sixty-seven, the oldest man ever elected President; first to actively campaign for himself with the first campaign slogan, "Tippecanoe and Tyler Too"; his rally at Tippecanoe drew 60,000 people, and songs such as "Good Hard Cider" and "The Gallant Old Hero" were written about him

* Inauguration speech was the longest to date—a full ninety minutes and 8,445 words, written by him and edited by Daniel Webster

* First U.S. President to die in office and first to lie in state in the Capitol

* Tried to do all that was expected of him as the country's leader, including trudging around Washington to purchase supplies for the White House.

• •

10. John Tyler
(1790–1862)
Presidency: 1841–1845 | One term | 19th century
Vice President: None (1841–1845)

"I contend that the strongest of all governments is that which is most free."

How He Defined the Office:

The first Vice President to succeed a President who had died in office, Tyler asserted he had the full power of the office, setting a precedent that has been followed ever since.

John Tyler

Accomplishments & Failures:

* Log Cabin Bill enabled settlers to claim 160 acres of land and later pay $1.25 an acre for it

* Annexation of Texas: followed it up by signing Texas statehood bill three days before leaving office

* First American President against whom impeachment process was initiated; process failed

* Established trade relationship with China not unlike what Britain had with China

* On Tyler's last day in office, Congress for the first time overrode a presidential veto of a bill, a bill designed to prevent the President from appropriating federal funds to build cutter ships without Congress's approval.

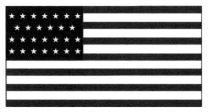

27-star American flag (Florida): 1845–1846.

James K. Polk

11. James K. Polk
(1795–1849)
Presidency: 1845–1849 | One term | 19th century
Vice President: George M. Dallas (1845–1849)

"One great object of the Constitution was to restrain majorities from oppressing minorities or encroaching upon their just rights."

How He Defined the Office:

Building on his campaign slogan "Fifty-Four Forty or Fight!," Polk made western expansion a priority.

Accomplishments & Failures:

* U.S. Department of the Interior established to manage the land acquired in Tyler's efforts to expand the United States from coast to coast

* Great Irish Potato Famine resulted in hundreds of thousands of Irish immigrants arriving on American shores

* Mexican-American War of 1846, also known as "Mister Polk's War"

* 1846 Oregon Treaty gave the United States Oregon, Washington, Idaho, and control of the Columbia River

* California Gold Rush

* 1848 Treaty of Guadalupe-Hidalgo ended Mexican-American war, leaving United States with what would become Arizona, California, Utah, Nevada, New Mexico, and part of Wyoming and Colorado; set the boundary of Texas at the Rio Grande.

. . . .

12. Zachary Taylor
(1784–1850)
Presidency: 1849–1850 | One partial term | 19th century
Vice President: Millard Fillmore (1849–1850)

"It would be judicious to act with magnamity towards a prostrate foe."

Zachary Taylor

How He Defined the Office:

Taylor served one year and had Congress handle most domestic matters; saw his role as vetoing laws he deemed unconstitutional.

Accomplishments & Failures:

* Apache Wars begin in 1849; continued until 1924

* Impeded Compromise of 1850 because he favored admission of California and New Mexico as free states

* Clayton-Bulwer Treaty recognized as an important step in scaling back the country's commitment to Manifest Destiny; signed with Britain; ensured any future canal across Central America would be open to all nations

* Died in office of indigestion after eating cherries; his untimely death led to rumors that he had been poisoned by proslavery southerners.

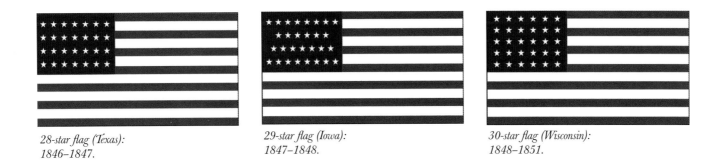

28-star flag (Texas):
1846–1847.

29-star flag (Iowa):
1847–1848.

30-star flag (Wisconsin):
1848–1851.

The 28-Star American Flag

The 28th star was added to the flag when the United States annexed Texas.
The annexation would spawn the Mexican-American War, the first war in which American troops carried Old Glory
into battle. The United States won the war, defeating Mexico, and gained the land that would one day
become New Mexico, Utah, Nevada, Arizona, California, and much of western Colorado.

James Polk was the only President to serve under this flag—just as he was the only President to serve
under the 27-Star and 29-Star flags. He also served under the 26-Star and 30-Star flags;
all in all, Polk served under five versions of the American flag during his tenure as President.

Millard Fillmore

13. Millard Fillmore
(1800–1874)
Presidency: 1850–1853 | One partial term | 19th century
Vice President: None (1850–1853)

"Liberty unregulated by law degenerates into anarchy, which soon becomes the most horrid of all despotism."

How He Defined the Office:
Fillmore filled the remaining term of Taylor; he detested slavery but believed that to save the country, a compromise was needed to provide a timeline for the resolution of the issue.

Accomplishments & Failures:
* Compromise of 1850 allowed newly formed territories of New Mexico and Utah to decide slavery question themselves; admitted California as a free state; and banned slave trade—but not slavery—in Washington, D.C.
* Oregon Gold Rush of 1851
* Apache Wars continued—along with Yuma War, Ute Wars, Mariposa Indian War
* White House Library established with 200 volumes, along with periodicals and government documents—previously Presidents brought their personal libraries and removed them at the end of their stay. Fillmore raced to help put out a December 1851 blaze at the Library of Congress and signed a bill to replace all the books destroyed in the fire.

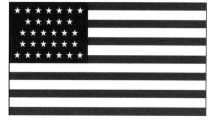
31-star American flag (California): 1851–1858.

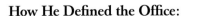

14. Franklin Pierce
(1804–1869)
Presidency: 1853–1857 | One term | 19th century
Vice President: William King (1853), None (1853–1857)

"With the Union my best and dearest earthly hopes are entwined."

Franklin Pierce

How He Defined the Office:
Pierce intended to solve the slavery issue but ended up laying the groundwork for civil war.

Accomplishments & Failures:
* Two months before Pierce took office, his eleven-year-old son was killed in a train wreck
* Gadsden Purchase of 1854 paid Mexico $15 million for what is now part of southern New Mexico and Arizona, settling old border dispute
* Kansas-Nebraska Act of 1854 repealed Missouri Compromise, leaving Kansas to determine whether it would be a slave or free territory
* Ostend Manifesto of 1854 stated that the United States could attack Cuba if Spain refused to sell it to the U.S.

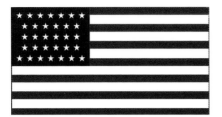

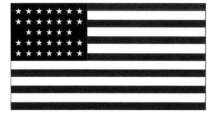

32-star American flag (Minnesota): 1858–1859.

33-star American flag (Oregon); the Civil War began on April 12, 1861, under this flag: 1859–1861.

15. James Buchanan
(1791–1868)
Presidency: 1857–1861 | One term | 19th century
Vice President: John C. Breckinridge (1857–1861)

"The ballot box is the surest arbiter of disputes among free men."

James Buchanan

How He Defined the Office:

This northern bachelor believed slavery was for states to decide. His inaction allowed the

Confederate government to rise as he served on the eve of the Civil War.

Accomplishments & Failures:

* Apache and Sioux wars continued

* Panic of 1857 led to major financial depression

* Supported Dred Scott Decision: March 6, 1857, the U.S. Supreme Court ruled that slaves were property and had no rights, and they were not and could never be citizens of the United States regardless of what state—free or slave—they lived in

* 1857–1858 Utah War, or Buchanan's Blunder: President sent troops to Utah to address "the Mormon problem"—ultimately not a shot was fired. As the *New York Herald* reported: "Killed, none; wounded, none; fooled, everybody."

* Harpers Ferry: In 1859, John Brown seized town of Harpers Ferry, Virginia, in attempt to spark slave uprising

* Wanted to annex Cuba and make it a slave territory

* Pony Express founded

* Secession of Six States: In December 1860, after Abraham Lincoln had been elected but Buchanan was still in office, South Carolina and six other states seceded from the Union. Buchanan did nothing for fear of provoking the South.

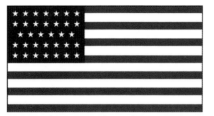

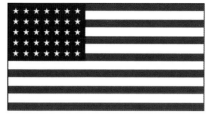

34-star American flag (Kansas):
1861–1863.

35-star American flag (West Virginia); Civil
War ended under this flag:
1863–1865.

The 34-star American Flag

Beginning with South Carolina on December 20, 1860, ten more states

(Mississippi, Florida, Alabama, Georgia, Louisiana, Texas, Arkansas, Tennessee,

North Carolina, and Virginia) had seceded from the Union by the summer of 1861.

President Lincoln refused to remove the stars representing those states from the American flag

because he believed the Southern states were still part of the nation. Some Northerners cut eleven stars

out of their own flags in protest. By year's end, Kentucky and Missouri had voted to secede.

Abraham Lincoln was the only president to serve under the 34-star American flag;

he also served under 33-star and 35-star flags.

16. Abraham Lincoln
(1809–1865)
Presidency: 1861–1865 | One term, one partial term | 19th century
Vice Presidents: Hannibal Hamlin (1861–1865), Andrew Johnson (1865)

"Nearly all men can stand adversity, but if you want to test a man's character, give him power."

Abraham Lincoln

How He Defined the Office:

Lincoln preserved the Union and by signing the Emancipation Proclamation, the country's moral center.

In refusing to even consider canceling elections in 1864 during the Civil War (despite it appearing he might not win), he cemented the role of Americans in deciding who should lead the country in good times and bad. It was the first time a democratic country had held a national election in a time of war.

Accomplishments & Failures:

* Inaugurated as the first Republican president, March 4, 1861
* Confederate States of America established by six slaveholding states—South Carolina, Mississippi, Florida, Alabama, Georgia, and Louisiana; grew to include eleven states
* Civil War: fought from April 12, 1861, to May 9, 1865
* April 19, 1861, proclaimed blockade of ports in Alabama, Florida, Georgia, Louisiana, Mississippi, South Carolina, and Texas
* Trent Affair of 1861 challenged doctrine of freedom of the seas and almost precipitated war with Great Britain
* February 20, 1862, the President's third son, William Wallace Lincoln, died at the age of eleven in a guest room in the White House
* U.S. Department of Agriculture established in 1862
* Homestead Act of 1862 approved, giving homesteads to settlers on government lands
* Pacific Railroad Act of 1862 provided federal support for the building of the first transcontinental railroad; completed May 10, 1869
* Morrill Land-Grant Act of 1862: also known as the Land Grant College Act, allowed for creation of land-grant colleges on the condition that the proposed institutions would also teach military tactics as well as engineering and agriculture
* Revenue Act of 1862 established the Office of the Commissioner of Internal Revenue, which later became the IRS, and introduced the progressive nature of income tax in the United States
* Gettysburg Address: announced dedication of part of Gettysburg battlefield as a national cemetery
* Emancipation Proclamation of 1863 signed, freeing all slaves in the rebellious states as of January 1, 1865
* National Banking Act of 1863 created U.S. national banking system and established a national currency
* 13th Amendment approved February 1, 1865; abolished slavery in the United States; ratified December 6, 1865
* 1863 Proclamation of Amnesty and Reconstruction announced Lincoln's intention to reunite the nation and reintegrate the conquered Southern States
* Assassinated April 14, 1865, by John Wilkes Booth during a play at Ford's Theatre, a month after Lincoln's reelection; died April 15, 1865, at age fifty-six.

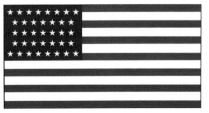

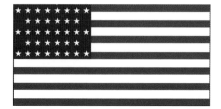

36-star American flag (Nevada): 1865–1867.

37-star American flag (Nebraska): 1867–1877.

Andrew Johnson

17. Andrew Johnson
(1808–1875)
Presidency: 1865–1869 | One partial term | 19th century
Vice President: None (1865–1869)

"Honest conviction is my courage; the Constitution is my guide."

How He Defined the Office:

Johnson survived the impeachment process and in doing so established the precedent that the U.S. Congress should not be able to remove a President from office simply because they disagree with or dislike the Commander in Chief.

Accomplishments & Failures:

* Reconstruction: recommended restoration of Confederate states to Union; granted amnesty to white southerners who took loyalty oath to United States
* Ku Klux Klan founded by white southern discontents December 24, 1865, in Pulaski, Tennessee; extended into almost every southern state by 1870; became a vehicle for white southern resistance to federal Reconstruction-era policies aimed at establishing political and economic equality for blacks
* Bureau of Refugees, Freedmen and Abandoned Lands Extension established in 1865 to help refugees of Civil War; Johnson vetoed the 1866 extension
* Civil Rights Act of 1866 mandated that "all persons born in the United States," with the exception of American Indians, were "hereby declared to be citizens of the United States"; vetoed by Johnson; veto overrode by House; granted all citizens the "full and equal benefits of all laws and proceedings for the security of person and property"
* Alaska Purchase of 1867 marked the end of Russian efforts to expand trade and settlements to the Pacific coast of North America and a step in the United State's rise as a power in the Asia-Pacific region; purchased for $7.2 million from the Russians; ensured U.S. access to the Pacific northern rim
* 14th Amendment ratified July 9, 1868; made every person born or naturalized in the United States a citizen and established constitutional provisions of "equal protection under the law" and the due process of law; opposed by Johnson
* First president impeached—acquitted by one vote.

18. Ulysses S. Grant

(1822–1885)
Presidency: 1869–1877 | Two terms | 19th century
Vice Presidents: Schuyler Colfax (1869–1873),
               Henry Wilson (1873–1875), none (1875–1877)

". . . There never was a time when, in my opinion, some way could not be found to prevent the drawing of the sword."

Ulysses S. Grant

How He Defined the Office:

Grant led an administration plagued by corrupt appointees—his tenure was plagued by scandal, although he was not implicated.

Accomplishments & Failures:

* Black Friday Scandal of 1869: led to collapse of U.S. gold market

* 15th Amendment ratified February 3, 1870; prohibited denying the right to vote based on race, color, or servitude

* First Ku Klux Klan Act of 1870 empowered President with legal authority to enforce first section of 15th Amendment

* Yellowstone Park founded 1872

* Whiskey Ring Scandal exposed in 1875 the diversion of tax revenues by agents, politicians, distillers, and distributors.

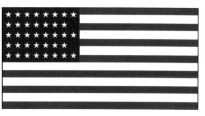

38-star American flag (Colorado): 1877–1890.

· ·

19. Rutherford B. Hayes

(1877–1881)
Presidency: 1877–1881 | One term | 19th century
Vice President: William Wheeler (1887–1881)

"The President of the United States should strive to be always mindful of the fact that he serves his party best who serves his country best."

Rutherford Hayes

How He Defined the Office:

Hayes oversaw no major national or international challenges but led a scandal-free administration.

Accomplishments & Failures:

* Great Railroad Strike of 1877 triggered by pay cuts to workers; Hayes sent federal troops to protect the mail and quell riots in many cities

* Compromise of 1877 ended Reconstruction; federal troops withdrew from South

* Civil Service Reforms of 1877 established merit-based process for appointments and promotion in federal jobs to end political-party "spoils system"

* In *U.S. ex rel. Standing Bear v. Crook*, May 12, 1879, Judge Elmer S. Dundy ruled "an Indian is a person" within the meaning of habeas corpus.

James Garfield

20. James A. Garfield
(1831–1881)
Presidency: 1881 | One partial term | 19th century
Vice President: Chester Arthur (1881)

"Next in importance to freedom and justice is popular education, without which neither freedom nor justice can be permanently maintained."

How He Defined the Office:

Garfield was in office 200 days—just shy of six months—but did manage to use his fiscal expertise to the benefit of the country.

Accomplishments & Failures:

* Recalled and refinanced government bonds, saving millions of dollars in the federal budget
* Star Route Scandal resulted in important civil service reforms after Garfield's investigation into claims that mail-route contracts were being awarded fraudulently revealed that his own party was involved in the scandal; nonetheless, he persevered
* Assassinated July 2, 1881, by Charles Guiteau for not getting a government post; second U.S. President to be assassinated
* Died September 19, 1881, from blood poisoning and complications from the shooting.

. . . .

21. Chester Arthur
(1829–1886)
Presidency: 1881–1885 | One term | 19th century
Vice President: None (1881–1885)

"There are very many characteristics which go into making a model civil servant. Prominent among them are probity, industry, good sense, good habits, good temper, patience, order, courtesy, tact, self-reliance. . . ."

Chester Arthur

How He Defined the Office:

Arthur hired New York City Designer Louis Tiffany to renovate White House but also worked to limit corruption in government appointments and civil service promotions. He oversaw the arrival of the *Statue of Liberty* from France.

Accomplishments & Failures:

* Geronimo's War
* Chinese Exclusion Act: banned Chinese citizenship, restricted Chinese immigration
* Immigration Act of 1882: restricted immigrants from Europe
* Pendleton Civil Service Reform Act: enacted in 1883; established a bipartisan Civil Service Commission; stipulated government appointments were to be based on merit and provided a "classified system" that made access to government positions obtainable only through competitive written examinations.

22. Grover Cleveland

(1837–1908)

Presidency: 1885–1889 | First of two nonconsecutive terms | 19th century

Vice President: Thomas Hendricks (1885), None (1885–1889)

"Your every voter, as surely as your Chief Magistrate, exercises a public trust. . . ."

Grover Cleveland

How He Defined the Office:

The only President to serve two nonconsecutive terms and to be married in the White House, Cleveland vetoed more bills in his first term in office than all previous Presidents combined; he also modernized the U.S. Navy.

Accomplishments & Failures:

* 1885 Board of Fortifications created to recommend a new coastal fortification system for the United States; led to twenty-seven locations being defended by more than seventy forts and included the transition from mortar to concrete building materials; these defenses, among others, remained in use until 1945

* Civil Rights Act of 1866 made blacks full U.S. citizens

* Presidential Succession Act of 1886 specified in the absence of a president and vice president, heads of executive departments would succeed to the presidency in the order in which the departments were created, starting with the secretary of state; remained in force until 1947

* *Statue of Liberty*: recommended to Congress the nation accept France's gift, which commemorated the alliance between the two countries during the Revolutionary War

* Interstate Commerce Act of 1887 required that railroad rates be "reasonable and just" and that railroads publicize shipping rates and prohibited fare discrimination that targeted smaller markets, particularly farmers; made railroad industry the first industry to fall under federal regulation

* Dawes Act of 1887divided tribal lands of Native Americans into individual allotments of 160 acres per family or eighty acres to single adults and forty acres to orphans and prohibited recipients from selling the land for a period of twenty-five years; encouraged the assimilation of Native Americans into American society; motivated in part by the demands of American settlers and railroads to reduce the quantity of land in tribal hands

* U.S. Department of Agriculture created in 1889.

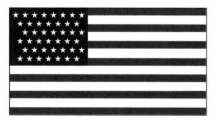

43-star American flag (North Dakota, South Dakota, Montana, Washington, Idaho): 1890–1891.

44-star American flag (Wyoming): 1891–1896.

23. Benjamin Harrison
(1833–1901)
Presidency: 1889–1893 | One term | 19th century
Vice President: Levi P. Morton (1889–1893)

"I pity the man who wants a coat so cheap that the man or woman who produces the cloth . . . will starve in the process."

How He Defined the Office:

Harrison expanded the U.S. Navy and through the McKinley Tariff, established presidential authority over foreign trade.

Benjamin Harrison

Accomplishments & Failures:

* Dependent Pension Bill of 1890 provided benefits to Union veterans and their children and widows
* Wounded Knee Massacre: December 29, 1890, barely a year after South Dakota became a state, some 300 Lakota men, women, and children died at Wounded Knee Creek in the last major military operation by the U.S. to subdue the Native American populations of North America
* Sherman Antitrust Act of 1890: first measure passed by Congress to prohibit trusts and monopolies
* Circuit Courts of Appeals created new courts to relieve the demands on the U.S. Supreme Court
* Forest Reserve Act of 1891 granted President ability to set aside unclaimed land for public domain, including America's first forest reserve in Wyoming.

. . . .

Grover Cleveland

24. Grover Cleveland
(1837–1908)
Presidency: 1893–1897 | Second of two nonconsecutive terms | 19th century
Vice President: Adlai E. Stevenson (1893–1897)

"A truly American sentiment recognizes the dignity of labor and the fact that honor lies in honest toil."

How He Defined the Office:

The only President to serve two nonconsecutive terms—his first from 1885 to 1889 as No. 22, Cleveland understood the presidency was a public trust bestowed upon him by the people.

Accomplishments & Failures:

* Panic of 1893 triggered by two railroads going bankrupt on May 4; the panic also distressed farm country
* Wilson-Gorman Tariff Bill of 1894 created an income tax of 2 percent on all personal income over $4,000 and on all corporate income above operating expenses; Cleveland refused to veto or sign but it became law anyway
* Illiteracy Ban of 1897: President vetoed bill that would ban illiterate immigrants.

45-star American flag (Utah): 1896–1908.

25. William McKinley
(1843–1901)

Presidency: 1897–1901 | One full term, one partial term | 19th to 20th centuries
Vice Presidents: Garret Hobart (1897–1899), none (1899–1901),
Theodore Roosevelt (1901)

"War should never be entered upon until every agency of peace has failed. . . ."

William McKinley

How He Defined the Office:

McKinley was a firm believer that the nation must adhere to the fundamental principles on which it was founded. His handling of thorny foreign policy decisions involving Cuba and with Spain helped set the United States up to be a force on the world stage.

Accomplishments & Failures:

* First Boston Marathon 1897

* 1897 Dingley Tariff Law raised custom duties an average of 57 percent—the highest tariff in U.S. history—just as the Depression of 1893 had almost run its course

* Spanish-American War: 100-day war saw U.S. destroy the Spanish fleet, seize Manila, Philippines, and occupy Puerto Rico

* Volunteer Army Act of 1898 organized first volunteer cavalry, known as the Rough Riders

* War Revenue Act of 1898 generated revenue from taxes levied on beer, tobacco, entertainment, and some businesses

* Treaty of Paris signed by the United States and Spain

* Championed market expansion, arguing, "It should be our settled purpose to open trade wherever we can, making our ships and our commerce messengers of peace and amity."

* Assassinated September 6, 1901, by Leon Czolgosz, an unemployed mill worker and professed anarchist; McKinley died eight days later from two gunshot wounds.

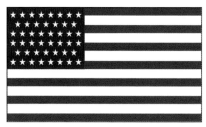

46-star American flag (Oklahoma):
1908–1912.

Theodore Roosevelt

26. Theodore Roosevelt
(1858–1919)
Presidency: 1901–1909 | One partial term, one full term | 20th century
Vice President: None (1901–1905), Charles Fairbanks (1905–1909)

"To educate a [person] in mind and not in morals is to educate a menace to society."

How He Defined the Office:

Youngest person to ever hold the office, he is considered the first modern president. He believed government could regulate big business to protect the interests of the people. As such he became famous for his Square Deal domestic program built on three basic ideas known as the "three Cs": conservation of natural resources, control of corporations, and consumer protection. In foreign policy, he believed America should "speak softly and carry a big stick."

Accomplishments & Failures:

* 1901 first family dines with African-American educator Booker T. Washington; first President ever to entertain an African-American in the White House
* Newlands Reclamation Act of 1902 authorized federal irrigation projects
* Coal Miners Strike of 1902 summoned striking Pennsylvania coal workers and mine owners to White House to settle strike
* Department of Commerce and Labor created in 1903 as ninth Cabinet office
* Elkins Act of 1903, Hepburn Act of 1906 curbed monopoly power of the railroads—Roosevelt would go on to destroy the Beef Trust as well
* *Champion v. Ames*: made federal power superior to that of the states
* Hay-Buneau-Varilla Treaty of 1903 gave the United States control of a ten-mile-wide canal zone for $10 million in gold and an annual fee of $250,000
* National Forest Services established in 1905
* *Jacobson v. Massachusetts*: recognized the legality of compulsory vaccination laws
* Antiquities Act of 1906 signed; Wyoming's Devils Tower becomes first National Monument
* 1906 Pure Food and Drug Act, Meat Inspection Act: banned food and drugs that were impure or falsely labeled from being made, sold, and shipped and required active ingredients be placed on label; latter prevented adulterated or misbranded meat and meat products from being sold and required sanitary conditions for the slaughter and processing of beef
* Awarded 1906 Nobel Peace Prize: first American so honored; given for leading the negotiations that ended the Russo-Japanese War of 1904–1905
* Square Deal Policy led to reforms to make business fair to all; led to trust-busting of big companies
* Spooner Act of 1902 authorized Panama Canal; Roosevelt considered its 1914 opening his most historically important international achievement
* U.S. Navy went from fifth largest to third largest in the world
* Started a tradition of conservatism of our public lands; President established the U.S. Forest Service, setting aside 125 million acres for national forests (more than all of his predecessors combined).

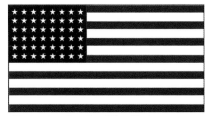

48-star American flag (New Mexico, Arizona): 1912–1959.

The 48-star American Flag

In 1912, President William Howard Taft passed an executive order establishing
the proportions for the American flag and the arrangement of the stars in six
horizontal rows of eight, with each star pointing upward. This flag was in service for
forty-seven years and through two World Wars, making it the longest serving flag
in American history until the record was usurped on July 4, 2007, by the
50-star American flag. That flag continues to fly today.

William H. Taft, Woodrow Wilson, Warren Harding, Calvin Coolidge,
Herbert Hoover, Franklin D. Roosevelt, Harry S. Truman, and
Dwight D. Eisenhower all served under this flag.

William Taft

27. William Howard Taft

(1857–1930)

Presidency: 1909–1913 | One term | 20th century

Vice President: James S. Sherman (1909–1912), none (1912–1913)

"Presidents come and go, but the Supreme Court goes on forever."

How He Defined the Office:

Promised to continue his predecessor's policies, but Taft got caught between progressives and conservatives. After his presidency, Taft was appointed to the U.S. Supreme Court by President Harding, becoming the only man to hold the highest position in both the executive and judicial branches of the U.S. government.

Accomplishments & Failures:

* Dollar Diplomacy: used diplomatic and military action on behalf of foreign business interests

* Payne-Aldrich Tariff Act lowered tariffs on certain goods entering the United States but not low enough to please Roosevelt and his supporters

* Postal Savings Depository Act established postal savings system

* 16th Amendment ratified February 3, 1913; authorized Congress to collect income taxes

* 17th Amendment ratified April 8, 1913; stated two senators elected by the people from each state would serve a six-year term.

• •

28. Woodrow Wilson

(1856–1924)

Presidency: 1913–1921 | Two terms | 20th century

Vice President: Thomas R. Marshall (1913–1921)

"America lives in the heart of every man everywhere who wishes to find a region where he will be free to work out his destiny as he chooses."

Woodrow Wilson

How He Defined the Office:

Wilson set the example for the modern activist President; a stroke in his last year left him half paralyzed.

Accomplishments & Failures:

* World War I: the "Great War" was first global war; originated in Europe; lasted from July 28, 1914, to November 11, 1918

* Selective Service Act required men between the ages of twenty-one and thirty to register for the federal draft lottery

* 18th Amendment ratified January 16, 1919; established Prohibition laws that banned sale, production, importation, and transportation of alcoholic beverages

* 19th Amendment ratified August 18, 1920; guaranteed women the right to vote.

Warren G. Harding

29. Warren G. Harding
(1865–1923)
Presidency: 1921–1923 | One partial term | 20th century
Vice President: Calvin Coolidge (1921–1923)

"Amercia's present need is not heroics, but healing; not nostrums, but normalcy; not revolution but restoration; . . . not surgery but serenity. . . ."

How He Defined the Office:

Having campaigned on a promise of a "return to normalcy," Harding considered the presidency largely ceremonial.

His administration was plagued with corruption; he is widely regarded as one of the worst presidents in American history.

Accomplishments & Failures:

* Emergency Quota Act of 1921 addressed massive influx of European immigrants at end of World War I

* Teapot Dome Scandal: bribery scandal from 1921 to 1923 that involved secret leasing of federal oil reserves by the Secretary of the Interior

* Sheppard-Towner Maternity and Infancy Act: in 1921, the President signed the act into law, funding maternity and infant health care

* Died of a heart attack August 2, 1923.

. . . .

30. Calvin Coolidge
(1872–1933)
Presidency: 1923–1929 | One partial term, one full term | 20th century
Vice President: None (1923–1925), Charles Dawes (1925–1929)

"The chief business of the American people is business."

How He Defined the Office:

Known as "Silent Cal," Coolidge addressed the nation by radio monthly and held many press conferences.

Calvin Coolidge

Accomplishments & Failures:

* Revenue Acts of 1924 and 1926 reduced inheritance and personal income taxes after wartime tax rates

* Immigration Act of 1924 ended immigration from Japan and restricted immigrants from southern and eastern Europe

* Air Commerce Act gave the commerce department regulatory power over sectors of the aviation industry

* 1924 Indian Citizenship Act gave citizenship to all Native American residents of the United States; their right to vote, however, was governed by the states, and some states barred Native Americans from voting until 1954.

31. Herbert Hoover

(1874–1964)
Presidency: 1929–1933 | One term | 20th century
Vice President: Charles Curtis (1929–1933)

"Older men declare war. But it is youth that must fight and die."

Herbert Hoover

How He Defined the Office:

Hoover entered office as the "Great Humanitarian" who fed war-torn Europe before and after World War I, only to become known for an economic crisis that put millions of Americans out of work and his failure to contain the Great Depression.

Accomplishments & Failures:

* Stock Market Crash of 1929: followed a boom that enticed many ordinary Americans to invest their entire savings in stocks
* Great Depression: worst economic downturn in the history of the industrialized world; lasted 1929 to 1939 and saw average income of American families drop 40 percent
* Bonus Army March: 15,000 World War I veterans marched to demand bonus promised to them for their service
* 20th Amendment ratified January 23, 1933; reduced time between election day and start of presidential, vice presidential, congressional terms
* 21st Amendment ratified December 5, 1933; repealed the 18th amendment that mandated nationwide Prohibition on alcohol.

· ·

32. Franklin D. Roosevelt

Franklin Roosevelt

(1882–1945)
Presidency: 1933–1945 | Three full terms, one partial | 20th century
Vice Presidents: John Nance Garner (1933–1941), Henry A.
Wallace (1941–1945), Harry S. Truman (1945)

"The test of our progress is not whether we add more to the abundance of those who have much; it is whether we provide enough for those who have little."

How He Defined the Office:

Remembered for the New Deal, which was enacted over eight years to lead the country out of the Great Depression, Roosevelt's unprecedented four terms speak to his popularity, but they also led to the future passage of the 22nd Amendment.

Accomplishments & Failures:

* Reduced rate of unemployment from 25 percent, the highest in the country's history, to 2 percent
* Civilian Conservation Corps: 1933 to 1942 public work relief program for unemployed unmarried men; millions worked on environmental projects

"I have seen war. I have seen war on land and sea. I have seen blood running from the wounded. I have seen men coughing out their gassed lungs. I have seen the dead in the mud. I have seen cities destroyed. I have seen two hundred limping, exhausted men come out of line—the survivors of a regiment of one thousand that went forward forty-eight hours before. I have seen children starving. I have seen the agony of mothers and wives. I hate war." —FDR

* Federal Emergency Relief Administration, Works Progress Administration: FERA replaced by WPA in 1935; WPA employed millions of unskilled men to carry out public works projects, including the construction of public buildings and roads

* 1933 National Industry Recovery Act created Civil Works Administration, a short-term program designed to help the jobless through the winter of 1933–1934—two months after its start, CWA had almost 4.3 million formerly unemployed workers on its payroll. CWA built forty-four thousand miles of new roads, two thousand miles of levees, one thousand miles of new water mains, four thousand new or improved schools, and one thousand new or improved airports; shuttered in 1934 but recreated in the form of the Works Progress Administration in 1935

* National Youth Administration provided work and education for Americans between the ages of sixteen and twenty-five

* 1933 Banking Act (also known as the Glass-Steagall Act) prohibited banks from engaging in the investment banking business as a response to the failure of nearly five thousand banks during the Great Depression and established the Federal Deposit Insurance Corporation, an independent agency created to main stability and public confidence in U.S. financial system by insuring deposits

* Tennessee Valley Authority established in 1933; provided jobs and electricity to rural Tennessee River Valley, an area that spans seven southern states; it remains the nation's largest public power provider

* Security and Exchange Commission created to enforce federal securities laws in the wake of the crash of 1929

* National Firearms Act of 1934: federal gun-control legislation; covered machine guns and short-barreled firearms, including sawed-off shotguns; imposed a tax on any transfers of such weapons; levied a $200 tax on the manufacture or sale of these two types of firearms, with all sales to be recorded in a national registry

* National Housing Act of 1934 created the Federal Housing Administration to set standards for construction and underwriting for home building

* Fair Labor Standards Act of 1938 set minimum wage, overtime pay eligibility, recordkeeping, and child labor standards for full- and part-time workers

* Social Security Act of 1935: created a social insurance program to pay retired works age sixty-five or older a continuing income after retirement

* World War II: served as commander-in-chief

* Lend-Lease Act: called a special session of Congress to change the United State's existing neutrality acts and allow Britain and France to purchase American arms on a "cash-and-carry basis" in an effort to help Great Britain defeat Nazi Germany

* Atlantic Charter: (with Britain's prime minister Winston Churchill) declared the Four Freedoms on which the postwar world should be founded: freedom of speech and expression, freedom of religion, freedom from want, and freedom from fear

* Fair Employment Practice Committee established first national program directed against employment discrimination; prohibited racial and religious discrimination in the national defense industry

* United Nations: Spent final years of his life working to create the United Nations and to ensure the United States would play an active role in it.

"Books can not be killed by fire. People die, but books never die. No man and no force can abolish memory. . . . In this war, we know, books are weapons. And it is a part of your dedication always to make them weapons for man's freedom." —FDR

Harry Truman

33. Harry S. Truman
(1945–1953)
Presidency: 1945–1953 | One partial term, one full term | 20th century
Vice President: None (1945–1949), Alben Barkley (1949–1953)

". . . America was not built on fear. America was built on courage, on imagination and an unbeatable determination to do the job at hand."

How He Defined the Office:
Truman oversaw the end of World War II, an undeclared war in Korea, and increased tensions with the Soviets in the Cold War.

Accomplishments & Failures:
* 1947 Truman Doctrine: crystallized American willingness to provide military aid to countries resisting communist insurgencies
* 1948–1951 Marshall Plan, or the European Recovery Program: $13 billion effort to help rebuild Western European economies following World War II
* 1948 Executive Order 9981 abolished discrimination "on the basis of race, color, religion, or national origin"
* 22nd Amendment ratified February 27, 1951; limited presidents to two terms
* 1949 North Atlantic Treaty Organization: built a military barrier to confront the Soviet-dominated part of Europe in the Cold War
* 1950–1953 Korean War: Never officially declared by Congress, it was Truman's response to communist North Korea invading South Korea.

· ·

34. Dwight D. Eisenhower
(1890–1969)
Presidency: 1953–1961 | Two terms | 20th century
Vice President: Richard Nixon (1953–1961)

"I hate war as only a soldier who has lived it can, only as one who has seen its brutality, its futility, its stupidty."

Dwight Eisenhower

How He Defined the Office:
Supreme Commander of the Armed Forces before he became President, Eisenhower as President focused on keeping world peace and adhered to a middle ground at home, with an emphasis on a balanced budget.

Accomplishments & Failures:
* *Brown v. Board of Education*: May 17, 1954, Supreme Court ruling desegregated public schools; President sent troops into Little Rock to ensure compliance
* Vietnam War: since the U.S. Congress never declared war against Vietnam, technically a conflict; started November 1, 1955
* Federal-Aid Highway Act of 1956 created Interstate Highway System
* 1958 National Aeronautics and Space Administration created independent agency responsible for civilian space program and aerospace research.

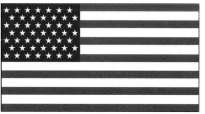
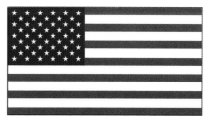

49-star American flag (Alaska):
1959–1960.

50-star American flag (Hawaii):
1960–present.

The 50-star American Flag

On July 4, 2007, the 50-star American flag became America's longest serving flag.

Dwight D. Eisenhower, John F. Kennedy, Lyndon B. Johnson, Richard M. Nixon, Gerald R. Ford, Jimmy Carter, Ronald W. Reagan George H.W. Bush, William J. Clinton, George W. Bush, Barack H. Obama, and Donald J. Trump all served under this flag.

· ·

35. John F. Kennedy
(1917–1963)
Presidency: 1961–1963 | One partial term | 20th century
Vice President: Lyndon B. Johnson (1961–1963)

". . . my fellow Americans: ask not
what your country can do for you—ask
what you can do for your country."

John Kennedy

How He Defined the Office:

The youngest man and first Roman Catholic to become President, Kennedy served an almost three-year tenure dominated by civil rights issues, Cold War challenges, and the conflict in Vietnam, which remained an undeclared war during his term.

Accomplishments & Failures:

* 1960 New Frontier Program raised funds for education, medical care for the elderly, and aid to rural regions, as part of federal fight against the recession

* 23rd Amendment ratified March 29, 1961; gave people in District of Columbia right to vote for President

* 1961 Peace Corps established to encourage Americans to volunteer, provide technical expertise to undeveloped countries, and promote cultural exchange

* 1961 Alliance for Progress aimed to establish economic cooperation between the United States and Latin America

* 1961 Bay of Pigs: CIA-financed and -trained group of Cuban refugees attempted to topple communist government of Fidel Castro; attack was a failure
* 1961 Apollo Program: President asked Congress to approve about $5 billion for the first space program to put a man on the moon and return the astronaut safely to earth
* Equal Pay Act of 1963 designed to eliminate wage discrepancies based on gender
* Nuclear Test-Ban Treaty of 1963 prohibited testing of nuclear weapons in outer space, underwater, or in the atmosphere by the United States, the United Kingdom, and Soviet Union
* Assassinated November 22, 1963, as his motorcade drove through Dallas, Texas. Lee Harvey Oswald was arrested for the shooting.

· ·

Lyndon Johnson

36. Lyndon B. Johnson
(1908–1973)
Presidency: 1963–1969 | One partial term, one full term | 20th century
Vice President: None (1963–1965), Hubert Humphrey (1965–1969)

"A man without a vote is a man without protection."

How He Defined the Office:

While dealing with the Cold War and escalating the U.S. presence in Vietnam, Johnson also focused on domestic policy and his goal of ending poverty and achieving racial equality in the United States to achieve the Great Society.

Accomplishments & Failures:

* Economic Opportunity Act of 1964 (part of Johnson's War on Poverty) established the Office of Economic Opportunity to oversee educational training programs for Americans
* 24th Amendment ratified January 23, 1964; ended the poll tax and made it illegal to make anyone pay a tax to have the right to vote
* Civil Rights Act of 1964, signed into law on July 2, 1964, prohibited discrimination in public places (swimming pools, libraries), provided for the integration of public schools and other public facilities, and made employment discrimination illegal—it was the most sweeping civil rights legislation since Reconstruction
* Voting Rights Act of 1965, signed into law on August 6, 1965, outlawed discriminatory voting practices adopted in many southern states after the Civil War, including literacy tests as a prerequisite to voting
* 25th Amendment ratified February 10, 1967; changed procedure if a president or vice president died, resigned, or was unable to do the job
* Vietnam War escalated troop levels from 3,500 in 1965 to 550,000 by 1968
* Civil Rights Act of 1968 defined housing discrimination as refusal to sell or rent a dwelling to a person because of race, color, religion, or national origin
* 1965 Medicare and Medicaid provided health care for the elderly and the poor.

37. Richard Nixon
(1913–1994)

Presidency: 1969–1974 | One full term, one partial term | 20th century
Vice President: Spiro Agnew (1969–1973), none (1973),
Gerald Ford (1973–1974)

*"The greatest honor
history can bestow
is the title of
peacemaker."*

Richard Nixon

How He Defined the Office:

First President to have a vice president resign in disgrace and first President to resign from office in lieu of impeachment—the latter stemming from the Watergate scandal. Nixon believed strong domestic policies could be based on strong foreign policy.

Accomplishments & Failures:

* Appointed four Supreme Court justices: Burger, Blackmun, Powell, and Rehnquist
* 1970 Environmental Protection Agency: created in 1970 to protect human health and the environment, it oversaw passage of the Clean Air Act, the Clean Water Act, and the Mammal Marine Protection Act
* 26th Amendment ratified July 1, 1971; lowered the voting age from twenty-one to eighteen years of age
* 1972 Title IX prevented gender bias at colleges and universities receiving federal aid
* 1972 Anti-Ballistic Missile Treaty calmed U.S.-Soviet tensions by curtailing the threat of nuclear weapons between the world's two superpowers
* 1972 Shanghai Communiqué signaled desire for normalized relations with China; agreement ended twenty-three years of diplomatic estrangement
* 1973 Draft ended; moved U.S. military to an all-volunteer force
* 1973 Paris Peace Accord ended U.S. involvement in the Vietnam conflict
* 1973 Menominee Restoration Act ended termination status of Native American tribes and restored their right to self-determination.

· ·

38. Gerald Ford
(1913–2006)

Presidency: 1974–1977 | One partial term | 20th century
Vice President: None (1974), Nelson Rockefeller (1974–1977)

*"I believe that truth is the
glue that holds government
together. . . . "*

Gerald Ford

How He Defined the Office:

Appointed to the post of vice president and then succeeded Nixon on August 8, 1974. On the thirty-first day of his presidency, Ford pardoned Nixon for any crimes he might have committed as President as part of what Ford called his efforts to unite the country.

Accomplishments & Failures:

* 1974 Federal Campaign Act Amendments of 1974 established bipartisan Federal Election Commission, among other reforms
* 1974 Freedom of Information Act Amendment: President vetoed bill saying it did not do enough to protect sensitive and classified documents; Congress overrode Ford's veto, making the bill law
* Privacy Act of 1974 established code of practices that governs collection, maintenance, use, and dissemination of information about individuals in records held by federal agencies; allowed individuals to examine records pertaining to them; required federal agencies to ensure accuracy of said records
* Two assassination attempts: September 5, 1975, Charles Manson follower Lynette "Squeaky" Fromme attempted to assassinate the President in Sacramento, California; on September 22 of the same year, Sara Jane Moore made an attempt on Ford's life in San Francisco
* Energy Policy Conservation Act of 1975: in the wake of 1973 oil crisis, created a comprehensive approach to federal energy policy
* Government in the Sunshine Act required government regulatory agencies to give advance notice of meetings and hold open meetings.

· ·

Jimmy Carter

39. Jimmy Carter
(1924–   )
Presidency: 1977–1981 | One term | 20th century
Vice President: Walter Mondale (1977–1981)

"Can we be both the world's leading champion of peace and the world's leading supplier of weapons of war?"

How He Defined the Office:

Carter brought honesty and high standards to the office of President but had difficulty dealing with Congress.

Accomplishments & Failures:

* 1977 Vietnam War Era Pardon: pardoned draft-evasion acts from August 4, 1964, to March 28, 1973
* Panama Canal Treaty of 1977 started process to return the Panama Canal to the Panamanians by the year 2000
* 1977 U.S. Department of Energy created; began tax incentives for home insulation and solar energy
* Ended federal price regulation of trucking, interstate buses, railroads, and airlines
* Phased out federal price controls for natural gas and then crude oil
* 1979 U.S. Department of Education established as a Cabinet-level agency
* Increased college tuition grants for needy students
* 1978 Camp David Accords brokered first Israel-Egypt peace treaty, one that remains in effect and laid groundwork for improved Israeli-Arab relations
* Iran Hostage Crisis: November 4, 1979, to January 20, 1981, fifty-two American diplomats and citizens held hostage 444 days at U.S. embassy in Tehran
* Established diplomatic relations with China, officially transferring U.S. diplomatic relations to mainland China.

40. Ronald Reagan
(1911–2004)
Presidency: 1981–1989 | Two terms | 20th century
Vice President: George Bush (1981–1989)

"If we love our country, we should also love our countrymen."

Ronald Reagan

How He Defined the Office:

The Reagan doctrine of peace through strength provided support to anticommunist insurgencies in Central America, Asia, and Africa, while the Reagan Revolution worked to reduce the reliance of the American people on government.

Accomplishments & Failures:

* Sixty-nine days after taking office, Reagan survived an assassination attempt; hospitalized for thirteen days after shooting
* 1983 Grenada Invasion: President ordered after deciding Marxist government posed threat to a thousand Americans, mostly students, on the island
* Tax Reform Act of 1986 simplified tax code by eliminating tax shelters and reducing number of deductions and brackets
* 1987 Iran-Contra Scandal: arms were traded for hostages and proceeds given to anti-communist Contra rebels in Nicaragua
* 1987 Intermediate-Range Nuclear Forces Treaty required United States and Soviet Union to eliminate nuclear and conventional ground-launched missiles.

. . . .

41. George H.W. Bush
(1924–   )
Presidency: 1989–1993 | One term | 20th Century
Vice President: Dan Quayle (1989–1993)

"Don't confuse being 'soft' with seeing the other guy's point of view. . . ."

George H.W. Bush

How He Defined the Office:

Bush was the first post-Cold War president and saw foreign challenges in the Middle East emerge again.

Accomplishments & Failures:

* 1989 Financial Institutions Reform, Recovery, and Enforcement Act responded to 1,043 of 3,234 savings and loan associations failing
* 1989 Panama Military Operation launched Operation Just Cause, sending tens of thousands of troops into Panama to execute an arrest warrant on dictator Manuel Noriega on charges of drug trafficking; Noriega went into hiding
* 1990 Americans with Disabilities Act prohibited discrimination in employment, state and local government, public accommodations, telecommunications
* 1990 Persian Gulf War launched thirty-nation coalition to free Kuwait following invasion by Iraqi dictator Saddam Hussein
* 27th Amendment ratified May 7, 1992; required no change in compensation for representatives or senators to take effect until an election has been held.

Bill Clinton

42. Bill Clinton

(1946–   )
Presidency: 1993–2001 | Two terms | 20th and 21st centuries
Vice President: Al Gore (1993–2001)

"There is nothing wrong with America that cannot be cured by what is right with America."

How He Defined the Office:

Clinton was the first Democrat to win back-to-back presidential terms since FDR. He oversaw the country's longest peacetime economic expansion, a record 115 months, while also balancing the federal budget and reducing the federal deficit.

Accomplishments & Failures:

* Family Medical Leave Act of 1993 required employers to provide employees with job-protected and unpaid leave for qualified medical and family reasons
* 1993 World Trade Center Bombing: six people killed and a thousand injured from bomb planted under World Trade Center in New York City
* National Performance Review appointed vice president to initiative to "reinvent government" by reducing number of federal employees and cutting federal spending as a percentage of the gross national product to levels unseen since Kennedy administration
* "Don't Ask, Don't Tell" allowed gay service members to serve in the military so long as they did not acknowledge their sexual orientation
* Brady Act required a potential handgun purchaser to wait five days while law-enforcement officers conducted a background check
* 1993 North American Free Trade Agreement eliminated most trade barriers among the United States, Canada, and Mexico, creating the world's largest free-trade zone
* 1993 Israeli-Palestinian Declaration of Principles
* 1994 Violent Crime Control and Law Enforcement Act funded hiring of 100,000 community police officers; extended death penalty to include more than fifty federal crimes; included Violence against Women Act, which addressed domestic violence, dating violence, sexual assault, and stalking by providing grants to states for programs that prevent violence against women
* Vietnam Trade Embargo: lifted on February 3, 1994, ending nineteen-year embargo against Vietnam; launched efforts by Vietnam to locate 2,238 Americans listed as missing in action since the Vietnam conflict
* Congressional Accountability Act of 1995 required Congress to adhere to same anti-discrimination rules in the workplace as exist in rest of U.S.
* Oklahoma City bombing of Alfred P. Murrah Federal Building on April 19, 1995: far-right militia sympathizer and antigovernment discontent Timothy McVeigh committed worst act of domestic terrorism in U.S. history—168 people died, including nineteen children attending a day-care center there
* Children's Health Insurance Program of 1997 covered uninsured children in families with modest incomes but ones too high to qualify for Medicaid
* Impeached December 19, 1998; acquitted February 12, 1999, on both articles of impeachment: perjury and obstruction of justice.

· ·

43. George W. Bush
(1946–   )
Presidency: 2001–2009 | Two terms | 21st century
Vice President: Dick Cheney (2001–2009)

"Every nation in every region now has a decision to make. Either you are with us or you are with the terrorists."

George W. Bush

How He Defined the Office:

Named President-elect after U.S. Supreme Court in a 5-4 ruling stopped recount of votes in several contested Florida counties. Bush responded to 9/11 attacks on September 11, 2001, and saw 2008 deliver the worst financial crisis since the Great Depression.

Accomplishments & Failures:

* Office of Faith-Based and Community Initiatives created by executive order; charged with working to ease regulations on religious charities and faith-based groups' efforts to tackle community issues involving the poor and disadvantaged

* 2001 Tax Cut signed $1.35 trillion tax cut into law that slashed income taxes across the board and provided for gradual elimination of estate tax

* 9/11 terrorist attack on New York City's Twin Towers, the Pentagon in Washington, D.C., and United Airlines Flight 93 led to War on Terror

* Afghanistan Military Operation: October 7, 2001, President Bush announced start of Enduring Freedom military operation in Afghanistan

* USA PATRIOT Act (acronym for Uniting and Strengthening America by Providing Appropriate Tools Required to Intercept and Obstruct Terrorism)

* 2002 Homeland Security Act created Department of Homeland Security in response to the 9/11 attack

* No Child Left Behind Act of 2002 offered states greater flexibility in spending federal education dollars; required standardized math and reading tests

* 2002 Bush-Putin Nuclear Treaty: the United States and Russia agreed to reduce their nations' nuclear arsenals by two-thirds over the next ten years

* March 13, 2003 Iraq War (Second Gulf War): after 8 p.m. deadline for Hussein to leave Iraq passes, Bush declared the United States was at war with Iraq; the military endeavor was never officially declared a war by Congress

* Medicare Prescription Drug, Improvement, and Modernization Act: President signed December 8, 2003—largest overhaul of Medicare in the public health program's thirty-eight-year history

* With his second term in 2005, President became just the fourth Republican president in American history to serve two full terms

* Hurricane Katrina: administration accused of negligence as storm breached levees in New Orleans; killed more than 1,800 people and left more than 400,000 homeless between August 29, 2005, and August 31, 2005

* 2008 bank bailout: Bush signed $700 billion bailout for failing bank assets, largest in U.S. history

* 2008 auto bailout: Bush signed $17.4 billion bailout for General Motors and Chrysler to help keep the two American auto manufacturers from going bankrupt.

Barack Obama

44. Barack Obama
(1961–)
Presidency: 2009–2017 | Two terms | 21st century
Vice President: Joe Biden (2009–2017)

". . . there's not a liberal America and a conservative America—there's the United States of America."

How He Defined the Office:

Country's first black, biracial president, Obama guided United States out of the worst economic crisis since the Great Depression.

Accomplishments & Failures:

* Oversaw auto industry bailout from January 2009 through December 2013; injected $62 billion—in addition to $17.4 billion from Bush administration—into GM and Chrysler (Ford didn't need funds but took them so as not to suffer by competing with subsidized companies), saving 2.2 million jobs

* January 22, 2009 signed executive order to close Guantánamo Bay detention camp, Cuba; met strong Congressional resistance; remains open as of 2018

* Reversed Bush administration torture policies two days after taking office in executive order banning CIA "enhanced interrogation techniques"

* January 29, 2009 signed Lilly Ledbetter Fair Pay Act; restored pay discrimination lost by Supreme Court's *Ledbetter v. Goodyear Tire & Rubber Co.* decision

* February 2009 American Recovery and Reinvestment Act provided $787 billion stimulus package to fund efforts to spur economic growth to right the economy—in constant dollars ARRA was larger than the New Deal, larger than the Marshall Plan, the biggest education reform bill since the Great Society, the biggest foray into industrial policy since FDR, the biggest expansion of antipoverty initiatives since Lyndon Johnson, the biggest infusion of research money ever, and by making most of George W. Bush's tax cuts permanent the biggest middle-class tax cut since Ronald Reagan

* October 9, 2009 awarded Nobel Peace Prize for being the rare person to capture the world's attention and give its people hope for a better future

* Hate Crimes Prevention Act of 2009 provided funding and technical assistance to state, local, and tribal jurisdictions to help them investigate and prosecute hate crimes

* Haiti aid: President pledged $100 million to assist Haiti in recovery from January 12, 2018, magnitude 7.0 earthquake

* 2010 Patient Protection and Affordable Care Act provided 20 million Americans with health care; lowered uninsured rate from 16 percent to 9 percent; forbade insurance plans from rejecting anyone, charging more, or refusing to pay for essential health benefits for any preexisting condition

* 2010 NASA proposed $6 billion to NASA budget over next five years to be used for space exploration

* 2010 Dodd-Frank Wall Street Reform and Consumer Protection Act reregulated the financial sector after its risky practices caused the Great Recession

* 2010 Volcker Rule (part of the Dodd Frank Act): Most historic tightening of U.S. bank regulations since the Great Depression; after being challenged by community banks, enacted July 21, 2015; restricted banks from engaging in certain speculative investments not in the best interest of their customers

* Economic Stimulus Bill created $800 billion stimulus package to help the economy recover

* Bank and Auto Industry Relief Program provided $700 billion to save U.S. auto industry and shore up financial institutions

* 2011 special forces raid on Osama Bin Laden: Navy SEALS attack resulted in death of Osama Bin Laden, the mastermind behind 9/11

* 2011 Repealed "Don't Ask, Don't Tell": ended 1990s-era restriction; formalized first military policy allowing gay persons to openly serve in military

* Iraq and Afghanistan wars: brought home 90 percent of the nearly 180,000 troops deployed from both war theatres

* 2015 Joint Comprehensive Plan of Action: President led a coalition of nations to an agreement with Iran to limit its nuclear program

* 2015 Paris Agreement: 197 nations agreed to goals to reduce global carbon emissions and limit global rise in temperature to 2 degrees Celsius.

· ·

45. Donald J. Trump
(1946–)
Presidency: 2017–present | 21st century
Vice President: Mike Pence (2017–present)

"Together, we will make America strong again. We will make America wealthy again. We will make America proud again. We will make America safe again. And, yes, together, we will make America great again."

Donald Trump

How He Defined the Office:
Embarked on a policy of "America First," as well as anti-immigration and anti-environmental protection policies, pro–Second Amendment gun freedom, sharply critical of NATO allies, and anti-free trade.

Accomplishments & Failures:
* Entered office with administration under Congressional and Department of Justice investigations with respect to collusion with Russian-sponsored interference in 2016 U.S. presidential election

* Exited the Trans-Pacific Partnership and the North American Free Trade Agreement, reversing decades of Republican support for free trade, ceding leadership in Asia and the South Pacific to China

* January 31, 2017, appointed Judge Neil Gorsuch of Colorado to the Supreme Court of the United States; commissioned April 8, 2017

* Embraced autocrats in Russia, Turkey, Saudi Arabia, Philippines, and Egypt, abandoning longtime U.S. leadership in democracy and human rights

* June 1, 2017, announced U.S. would cease all participation in the 2015 Paris Agreement on climate change, joining Syria and Nicaragua

* Failed to repeal the Affordable Care Act

* September 20, 2017, oversaw slow, flawed response to Hurricane Maria in Puerto Rico and U.S. Virgin Islands (territories' citizens are U.S. citizens). Parts of Puerto Rico went without power for more than a year; government death toll estimates rose from 64 initially to 2,975 by late August 2018

* December 22, 2017, Tax Cuts and Jobs Act cut corporate rate from 35 to 21 percent, dropped individual top tax rate to 37 percent, doubled standard deduction, and eliminated personal exemptions—individual changes/reductions to expire in 2025, corporate changes/reductions to be permanent

* May 7, 2018, adopted "zero-tolerance policy" for illegal border crossings resulted in the separation of more than 2,000 children from their parents

* June 12, 2018, convened summit with North Korea's Supreme Leader Kim Jong-un in Singapore, with a goal of denuclearization of Korean peninsula

* July 16, 2018, convened summit with Russian President Vladimir Putin; press conference afterward left Trump siding with Russian on election meddling.

ORHAN CAM / SHUTTERSTOCK.COM

"(The White House) is the 'People's House.' It's a place that is steeped in history, but it is also a place where everyone should feel welcome."

—First Lady Michelle Obama

The Appeal

Honor and preserve our Constitution and the Bill of Rights, for these are the cornerstones of our nation's values and purposes. These principles were born of the genius of our founders, preserved by so many who gave their lives to sustain them, and adopted by all who have come to our country seeking the opportunity to be a part of, and live their lives in accordance with, them. These principles constitute our collective moral and social ethic, and now more than ever, they require your vigilant support.

Believe in our nation and in the extraordinary principles which have permitted a multiethnic, multiracial, multicultural, religiously diverse population to live together as fellow Americans.

Honor those who have died, those who have been injured, and those who are still fighting to preserve these principles. The world has clearly grown more cynical—all the more reason to not let those who are cynical and self-serving distort or compromise our purposes as a nation, domestically and internationally. Do not permit cynicism to corrode or corrupt our values.

Believe in our flag and the principles it stands for: freedom, justice, equality, and opportunity; it is more than essential, it is critical. Be wary of those who would violate our collective principles in the name of preserving them or justifying their political purposes.

We are a young nation with an extraordinary legacy, grounded in our founding documents: the Declaration of Independence, the Constitution, the Bill of Rights, and the other amendments to the Constitution. Why would we not want to believe in them and put them to work for America?

Believe in the truth.

Words To Remember from
American writers, philosophers, legislators, and presidents

". . . loyalty to the Nation *all* the time, loyalty to the Government when it *deserves* it."
—Mark Twain, author

"My country, right or wrong; if right, to be *kept* right; and if wrong, to be *set* right."
—Carl Schurz

"Human kindness has never weakened the stamina or softened the fiber of a free people.
A nation does not have to be cruel in order to be tough."
—Franklin D. Roosevelt

"A people that values its privileges above its principles soon loses both."
—Dwight D. Eisenhower

"To announce that there must be no criticism of the President, or that we are to stand by the President,
right or wrong, is not only unpatriotic and servile, but is morally treasonable to the American public."
—Theodore Roosevelt

"How can we love our country and not love our countrymen; and loving them,
reach out a hand when they fall, heal them when they're sick, and provide opportunity to make
them self-sufficient so they will be equal in fact and not just in theory?"
—Ronald Reagan

"The people—the people—are the rightful masters of both Congresses, and courts—not to
overthrow the Constitution, but to overthrow the men who pervert it. . . ."
—Abraham Lincoln

"Democracy is not so much a form of government as a set of principles."
—Woodrow Wilson

"I would not be the mere President of a Party. . . .
I should feel bound to administer the government untrammeled by party schemes."
—Zachary Taylor

"No man has a good enough memory to be a successful liar."
—Abraham Lincoln

"It is a paradox that every dictator has climbed to power on the ladder of free speech.
Immediately on attaining power each dictator has suppressed all free speech except his own."
—Herbert Hoover

"America is never wholly herself unless she is engaged in high moral principle. We as a people
have such a purpose today. It is to make kinder the face of the Nation and gentler the face of the world."
—George H.W. Bush

"When you single out any particular group of people for secondary citizenship status,
that's a violation of basic human rights."
—Jimmy Carter

"One isn't necessarily born with courage, but one is born with potential. Without courage, we cannot
practice any other virtue with consistency. We can't be kind, true, merciful, generous, or honest."
—Maya Angelou

"I could never lend myself to any transaction, however respectable,
that would commercialize on the prestige and dignity of the office of the Presidency."
—Harry Truman

"We should do everything we can to make sure this country lives up to our children's expectations."
—Barack Obama

More Words To Ponder

"If we could just send the same bunch of men to Washington for the good of the nation and not for political reasons, we could have the most perfect government in the world."

—Will Rogers

"I hate war with all my guts. But I admire the guys with guts enough to fight them when they have to be fought."

—Bob Hope

"Never be afraid to raise your voice for honesty and truth and compassion, against injustice and lying and greed. If you . . . will do this . . . you will change the earth."

—William Faulkner

"Without enough wilderness America will change. Democracy, with its myriad personalities and increasing sophistication, must be fibred and vitalized by regular contact with outdoor growths—animals, trees, sun warmth and free skies—or it will dwindle and pale."

—Walt Whitman

"The world will not be destroyed by those who do evil, but by those who watch them without doing anything."

—Albert Einstein

"I have a dream that my four little children will one day live in a nation where they will not be judged by the colour of their skin, but by the content of their character."

—Martin Luther King Jr.

"If we ever pass out as a great nation, we ought to put on our tombstone: 'America died from a delusion that she had moral leadership.' "

—Will Rogers

The Conclusion

We have always been a great nation.
With this book, it is my hope that in the remembering and rediscovery
of what it means to be an American, we will all become unabashed patriots,
mindful of our sacred duty to revere and preserve our great nation.

Acknowledgments

Appreciation to Mr. James J. Kaufman of Downstream Publishing,
for his thoughtful guidance, encouragement, and support, but especially for his friendship.
To Jeanne Devlin, whose creativity and hard work significantly enhanced this book.
To Patricia Kaufman, for her tireless efforts to make this book all it could be.
To Mr. Thomas Hilley, for the beautiful, hand-drawn presidential portraits that grace this work.

And to all the Americans who have gone before,
whose love of country and service to this grand experiment in democracy have given us
the America we all know and love.

Resources

AF.mil · Army.mil · Britannica.com · LATimes.com · Marines.mil · Monticello.org · National Archives, Washington, D.C. · Navy.mil · NPS.gov · Presidential Libraries and Museums of the National Archives · Project Gutenberg · Star-News, Wilmington, N.C. · State Historical Society of Iowa, The Annals of Iowa · The American Presidency Project, a nonprofit and nonpartisan online resource housed at the University of California, Santa Barbara · The Library of Congress, Presidents of the United States · The Miller Center, a nonpartisan affiliate of the University of Virginia · USCG.mil · USHistory.org · WhiteHouse.gov · WillRogers.com

For a full list of sources, as well as interesting notes on the various topics covered,
please visit www.AmericanBeautyAReminder.com.